THE EVOLUTION OF LAW AND THE STATE IN EUROPE

Most books about public power and the state deal with their subject from the point of view of legal theory, sociology or political science. This book, without claiming to deliver a comprehensive theory of law and state, aims to inform by offering a fresh reading of history and institutions, particularly as they have developed in continental Europe and European political and legal science. Drawing on a remarkably wide range of sources from both Western and Eastern Europe, the author suggests that only by knowing the history of the state, and state administration since the twelfth century, can we begin to comprehend the continuing importance of the state and public powers in modern Europe. In an era of globalization, when the importance of international law and institutions frequently lead to the claim that the state either no longer exists or no longer matters, the truth is in fact more complex. We now live in an era where the balance is shifting away from the struggle to build states based on democratic values, towards fundamental values existing above and beyond the borders of nations and states, under the watchful gaze of judges bound by the rule of law.

T0315818

The Evolution of Law
and the State in Europe

Seven Lessons

Spyridon Flogaitis

·HART·
PUBLISHING
OXFORD AND PORTLAND, OREGON
2017

Hart Publishing
An imprint of Bloomsbury Publishing Plc

Hart Publishing Ltd
Kemp House
Chawley Park
Cumnor Hill
Oxford OX2 9PH
UK

Bloomsbury Publishing Plc
50 Bedford Square
London
WC1B 3DP
UK

www.hartpub.co.uk
www.bloomsbury.com

Published in North America (US and Canada) by
Hart Publishing
c/o International Specialized Book Services
920 NE 58th Avenue, Suite 300
Portland, OR 97213-3786
USA

www.isbs.com

HART PUBLISHING, the Hart/Stag logo, BLOOMSBURY and the
Diana logo are trademarks of Bloomsbury Publishing Plc

First published in hardback, 2014
Paperback edition, 2017

British Library Cataloguing-in-Publication Data
A catalogue record for this book is available from the British Library.

ISBN: HB: 978-1-84946-644-8
PB: 978-1-50991-299-5

Typeset by Compuscript Ltd, Shannon
Printed and bound in Great Britain by
Lightning Source UK Ltd

To find out more about our authors and books visit www.hartpublishing.co.uk. Here you will
find extracts, author information, details of forthcoming events and the option to sign up for our
newsletters.

In Memory of
Professor Sir David Williams
scholar and policy maker

FOREWORD

It is an honour to contribute a foreword to this important, even unique, book. In it, Professor Flogaitis offers a panoramic view of the development of the state in Europe over thousands of years. He identifies the cultural underpinnings of the state from Hellenism to the rule of law, democracy to globalism. Using his great knowledge of history, political theory, international law and comparative public law, and his familiarity with the literature of his subject in English, French, German, Greek and Italian, he shows how ideas, social structures and institutions interacted to shape the evolution of the state from pre-feudal to post-modern forms. To achieve this in a small book is a great achievement. Not only has Professor Flogaitis encapsulated the ideas developed during his distinguished academic career, but he has also made available to Anglophone students and scholars of public law the ideas of scholars (including himself) which had been published in other European languages.

Professor Flogaitis is extraordinarily, perhaps uniquely, well placed to illuminate the way in which European states became significant, changed their forms, cemented notions of legal regularity within themselves, and adapted to the rise of supranational and international institutions exercising political and legal authority. He has studied and taught in many countries, always immersing himself in the history and social and legal culture of the place. His linguistic ability is remarkable, and this has allowed him to foster contact and dialogue between public lawyers throughout Europe and beyond, not least as co-founder of the European Group of Public Law (now the European Public Law Organization). In addition, he has experience beyond the academy, having exercised important political functions in the Greek state, conducted a private practice in Athens, and served as President of the United Nations Administrative Tribunal.

The result of this combination of expertise, experience and long reflection is a book which is concentrated yet accessible, illuminating and thought-provoking. One might ask why one should be interested in the state today. We are regularly told that we are now in a world where everything is globalised, or at least internationalised. Is it still useful to study the state when so much that happens within states depends on, and is sometimes controlled by, decisions made and events occurring outside the territory over which the state has little or no influence? The answer, I think, is that it is more important than ever to understand the working of states. There are three reasons for this.

First, the so-called 'international community' is a community of states. The more active the international community becomes, the more important it is to comprehend the respective roles and capabilities of states and the institutions through which they work domestically and collaborate with each other internationally.

Secondly, the international community itself sees states as essential to the effectiveness and legitimacy of international law. International institutions lack sufficient resources to impose their will on states, so international law and diplomacy can work only if there are states strong enough to create and maintain the conditions for orderly social life within their territories. This is shown by the emphasis which the United Nations and other international agencies place on state-building in troubled areas such as Iraq, Sudan, Afghanistan, Kosovo, and Bosnia and Herzegovina.

Thirdly, and most significantly, people need states which operate close to them and are responsive to them. It is not enough to be controlled by distant decision-makers without direct responsibility for conditions in one's own part of the world. Experience of what are sometimes called 'failed states' shows that Thomas Hobbes did not exaggerate the evils which flow from the absence of Leviathan. Nevertheless, contrary to Hobbes's argument, maintaining basic conditions for personal security does not necessitate absolutism or lack of accountability of state institutions. Different structures, embodying different political and constitutional ideals and forms, are capable of providing a reasonable level of security. As Professor Flogaitis shows, states manifest a variety of conceptions of the separation of powers, the rule of law and democracy, which reflect differing social, political and legal cultures. With luck, each state develops in ways which are in tune with the prevailing cultures in its society, thus underpinning its own legitimacy and the security of its people.

For these (and no doubt other) reasons, understanding how states work and grow is of at least as much practical importance now as it has ever been. It is also of cultural importance: the form of our state is evidence of our history and our current political ideals. Professor Flogaitis gives us an opportunity to reflect on our states in the light of the experiences and ideas which grew out of, and informed, others, allowing us to see ourselves more clearly. I am sure that I will not be the only reader who enjoys these benefits from this work by a great scholar of, and ambassador for, public law.

David Feldman
Rouse Ball Professor of English Law, University of Cambridge
31 May 2014

Preface

There have been many studies about public powers and the state in all jurisdictions of the world, especially in Europe and North America. The majority of them deal with both from the points of view of legal theory, sociology, political science and anthropology. There are others which adopt a legal approach and several among those are known for their contribution to the development of legal thought. The Germans and Austrians introduced the *Staatslehre* and the *Politologie* into legal teaching and dialogue, and the same traditions can be found – even less intensively – in every continental European country.

This book aims to contribute to the knowledge of public powers and the state, without wishing to be a comprehensive theory of law and state. It tries to bring together another reading of history and institutions, in order better to conceive both public powers and the state in their real dimensions, especially through the experiences and developments of continental European legal science.

My studies in both law and history in my early scientific years, gave me opportunities for exposure to two worlds and the relationship between them which is not necessarily fully acknowledged and explored. Historians often explore culture in a discreet manner, and their research findings and knowledge is not communicated to other disciplines and in particular, to lawyers. Public powers are, however, living institutions, evolving with time and therefore lawyers and historians need each other; the lawyers cannot approach and understand certain institutions without their historical dimension, and historians cannot, by the same reckoning, understand the institutions which may be the object of their research, without being enlightened to law. This simple truth is even more obvious in the area of so-called Byzantine studies, because most of the existing sources are legal documents of all sorts, which should not be read from the linguistic, but rather from the legal point of view, in order to be understood. Moreover, as a field of study in universities and research centres, history often suffers from scientific conventions inherited from the times. These are difficult to circumvent in the closed world in which historians work and live.

My background as a lawyer from Greece, who has studied, taught and lived for many years in Western Europe, has helped me understand how little scholarship is linked between these two worlds – those of geographically Western and Eastern Europe – which both share the same cultural heritage. Through the construction of their cultures, each draws from the same perception of history; yet our understanding of this is rendered partial by an ancient rift. It is as if the distrust and rejection between the Catholics and the Orthodox, the ascending European West and the declining European East, never ceased. So, I decided to re-examine this relationship.

Throughout this study, I frequently mention Massimo Severo Giannini, with the result that this book begins to take the shape of a kind of dialogue with his thought and teaching. He was a professor who marked his times, the legal science of the post-Second World War period; a man who was the son of continental European legal science, mainly Italian, German and French. At the same time, Giannini was exposed to English law; he was one of the very few of his generation who read extensively English law and this facilitated his understanding of English institutions. He was, moreover, a lawyer who knew how to combine sociology and political science with law without betraying the strictness of the legal doctrine.

I had the chance to be his disciple and had him as one of the directors of my doctoral studies (which was mainly directed by Professor Jean Rivero in Paris) and profited from both his science and kindness. His scientific work in the domain of the public powers and the state remains unparalleled although it has been further extended by his disciple par excellence Sabino Cassese, following the major developments of the last 20 years. Unlike Giannini – who wrote mainly in Italian or Spanish – Cassese also wrote extensively in English and in French.

My personal writings, mostly in Greek or French, have, since my early doctoral studies, married the concept of state and the articulation of public powers in many ways. Although my studies vary from the organization of public powers to administrative action and public contracts, all of them had a covert objective – to explore and understand public power from the perspective of various aspects of the existence of the state. In this *iter*, I was helped by the teaching that I received by the director of my doctoral studies in history, Professor Nicolas Svoronos, one of the most renowned personalities of recent times in Byzantine studies, who had a unique identity as a historian in understanding the legal institutions as well as a global vision of history. My historical understanding was galvanized in the many unforgettable discussions he so graciously offered me in the café Escorial of the Place de la Sorbonne after his seminars, as it was the custom in certain circles in Paris during the1970s. I also profited throughout my career from the writings and support of the great lawyer and friend, Sabino Cassese, who has always been one step ahead of any other of our times in exploring new dimensions in the science of public law.

I think therefore that this is the time and place to remember and pay tribute to all those who have been my professors or friends and who contributed, in one way or another, to forming my way of thinking as a public lawyer throughout the many years which have led to the writing of this book, on the basis of my teaching as Arthur Goodhart Professor of Legal Science in the Faculty of Law of the University of Cambridge. My good professors or friends – Jean Rivero, Massimo Severo Giannini, Nicolas Svoronos, Sabino Cassese, Sir William Wade, Sir David Williams, Eberhard Schmidt-Aßmann, Giuliano Amato – there is something from all of you in this book.

Last but not least, I want to express my gratitude to the Faculty of Law of the University of Cambridge, with first thanks due to Professor David Feldman, for having proposed me for this prestigious professorship. I am grateful, not only for the honour but also for the opportunity to be with them for the best part of an academic year and – still more – to teach their students, an excellent composition of lawyers from all over the world. Their interventions and remarks have contributed greatly in the writing of this book and I am thankful to them for an unforgettable experience.

Cambridge, Wolfson College, 18 June 2013

ACKNOWLEDGEMENTS

This book constitutes my first comprehensive attempt to communicate with the world of English-speaking legal science, my previous major books having been published in Greek or French. The resulting work owes a great deal to my friends, worldwide distinguished scholars or former students of mine at the University of Athens. Each has taken their own path in legal science after having spent their best years in some of the most renown Universities of France, Germany, Italy, the United Kingdom and the United States of America. All had the kindness to read my manuscript and make various suggestions. I feel the need, therefore, to thank them for their time and expertise. They include David Feldman, Rouse Ball Professor of English Law, University of Cambridge, Christos Rozakis, Professor of Public International Law, University of Athens, and former Vice-President of the European Court of Human Rights, Jean-Bernard Auby, Professor of Public Law, Sciences Po, Nikoletta Giantsi, Professor of History, University of Athens, Charalambos Anthopoulos, Professor of Constitutional Law, Free Open University of Greece, George Dellis, Professor of Public Law, University of Athens and Dr George Dimitropoulos, Max-Planck Institut in Luxembourg. Their suggestions have been invaluable. It does not need to be said that any misunderstandings are mine.

Equal thanks are due to Dr Kirsty Byrne, who proofread the book several times and invested in it her command of English. I am most indebted for all her efforts and comments.

This book, however, owes even more to the support and understanding that I have had from my wife Fay and especially from my teenage children, Ioannis and Constantinos, who – at such a delicate stage of their lives – missed me during my extended stay in Cambridge. I know that they now understand what they could not grasp when they were younger, that scientific knowledge and work demands sacrifices of all sorts, but that the satisfaction gained by the feeling of being part of it is unparalleled. As they are taking their first steps towards augmenting their own scientific knowledge, I only wish that opportunities arise for them to serve the development of knowledge to the best of their abilities.

Cambridge, Wolfson College, 12 May 2014
Spyridon Flogaitis

CONTENTS

Lesson 1

From the Roman Empire to the Rebirth of Public Powers in Europe[1]

The state is a concept of continental Europe. It gradually emerged as both reality and legal concept from the last centuries of feudalism. The conception of the national state ran parallel with the abandonment of the Imperial dream of various rulers throughout Europe.

The state has specific characteristics: it constitutes a certain way of organizing the political life of a given population, its central characteristic being the development of a hierarchical and well organized administration.[2] Such organization of political life is not eternal, but evolves together with the life of a given society and – beyond that – with the evolution of international realities.

In order to understand the birth of states, we need to turn our attention to the history of Europe, Europe being the cradle of modern organizational schemes internationally.

The Greeks conceived all concepts and values of modern civilization and proposed a specific way of developing the human character and community life. They

---

[1] This chapter constitutes an attempt to bring together pieces of knowledge and results of research conducted in recent times in several disciplines by scholars around the world and the European Public Law Organization. This international organization has already organized two international conferences and has an ongoing research project bringing together historians and lawyers around the thematic of this chapter. Antagonisms, misconceptions, political fighting of all sorts, religious passion and hatred in a Europe which was taking shape for more than 1,000 years after barbaric invasions, have hidden or misinterpreted truths and transparent situations, political realities and institutional cross-fertilizations and so on. Europe is, however, finally united again, through the European Union and the 28 nations which compose it today. Europe in its fledgling state, composed of six founding nations was the Empire of Charlemagne, the remembrance, in historical terms, of an act of division of the peoples of the continent in two Empires. In today's Europe, we need to rediscover the past, which is inevitably reflected in the institutions of today. What it teaches is of the lent decline of the Roman Empire which survived up to 1453 and was equalled, and indeed largely conditioned, by a lent uprising of the nations emerging in the lost territories of the Roman Empire in the rest of Europe and beyond. In one way, the one conditioned the other, but there is now evidence that the culture has always been one and the same and that the new powers and societies were only the continuation, perhaps in new forms, of a dying Roman Empire. On these issues see extensively: S Flogaitis and A Pantelis (eds), *The Eastern Roman Empire and the Birth of the Idea of State in Europe,* European Public Law Series, Vol LXXX (London, Esperia, 2005); also under print, European Public Law Organization, *The Presence and Contribution of the (Eastern) Roman Empire in the Formation of Europe,* European Public Law Series (Athens, European Public Law Organization, forthcoming).

[2] This is a commonly accepted principle, especially since the times of Max Weber, *Wirtschaft und Gesellschaft* (1922) (Tübingen, Mohr (Siebeck), 1976). See, among others, MS Giannini, *Il pubblico potere, Stati e amministrazioni pubbliche* (Bologna, Il Mulino, 1986).

proved themselves in absorbing lessons and elements originating in other, neighbouring civilizations. These they were able to re-adapt to suit their own societal characteristics and realities. They did this with pride, as they always considered it very important to learn from others.[3]

The World becomes Roman

The Greeks were the originators of modern political systems,[4] especially because they proposed individualism;[5] by this I mean the idea that the man constitutes an absolute value. This led to the concept of equality, because if all men constitute absolute values, then they are equals. This in turn led to egalitarianism, which is the basis of democracy. However, our civilization is Greco–Roman, not just Greek, because it was the Romans who created legal science and developed the art of government. The specific characteristics of law and practice which led to the concept of state were developed by the Romans, and were consolidated into systems leading to the concept of state by the late Roman Empire of Constantinople.[6]

The old civilizations which were politically organized around a central power, especially the civilizations of Mesopotamia, produced a bureaucracy which was a hierarchical organization dealing with administration, or parts of it. In most cases, these were administrations dealing with water resources and irrigation systems, on which the political power of the King was based. A system of tax collection was also administered; the taxes were important for the functioning of the political system and the maintenance of an army. Egypt was the best-known example of such a political system.[7]

The Greeks developed their political systems and invented monarchy, oligarchy, tyranny, aristocracy and democracy: all are Greek words and concepts.

---

[3] Solon is reported to have visited Egypt over many years and to have learned from the Egyptian priests; Herodotus travelled extensively and gives excellent accounts of the societies, customs and systems of government, especially those of Persia; Pythagoras was a student of the priests of Egypt; and so on.

[4] Except dictatorship, this was a Roman institution. The dictator was called upon by the Romans to address difficult political situations with exceptional powers within a limited period of time and thus help democracy function again.

[5] Individualism defined the Greeks until modern times. However, it also needs to be acknowledged that the expansion of the Greek civilization was largely due to the democratization of knowledge. Unlike other ancient civilizations, where knowledge was a secret shared by a few (for example, by the priests in Egypt), in Greece, knowledge was widely disseminated through education of all kinds and a belief in value per se.

[6] The so-called Byzantium, a term which is avoided in this study, for the simple reason that Byzantium never existed; the Emperor had the title of Roman Emperor and his people were called Romans until the end of their Empire. Modern historians use Byzantium as an established term and in this way they give the impression that this Empire was different from the Roman Empire. Thus, they have fed the confusion about the end of the western Roman territories tying in with the end of the Roman Empire.

[7] Giannini, *Il pubblico potere*, above n 2 at 27.

However, the Greek political systems did not produce bureaucracy – that is, an organized and well-developed administration – nor did the classical Romans, who mirrored the Greeks in functioning on the basis of offices–organs.

Unlike the Greeks or Romans, the Persians created a vast kingdom on the basis of a powerful and well-organized administration, obeying regional officials, the Satraps, and, through them, the all-powerful King. When the *epigones* of Alexander the Great founded and ruled their Hellenistic kingdoms, they inherited the bureaucracy of the former Persian Satraps, structures which they did not destroy. Consequently, when the Romans came, they did not destroy those structures either. Furthermore, sometimes they respected local rulers on the condition that they respected and obeyed Rome in return.

Octavian became *Princeps* and *Augustus* and the way was opened for monarchical ideas to enter the Roman system of governance. In time, the *Princeps* became *Imperator*, as it was an absolute political necessity to avoid the use of the term 'King' or 'Basileus', as these were titles condemned by Roman history. The *Imperator* became *Despotus* under the influence of Christianity.

By the middle of the second century BC the Romans had conquered the Italian peninsula; they then continued with the conquest of Greece and, gradually, of the rest of the Hellenistic world. This ultimately lost its political autonomy and was integrated in an empire governed by others.

The year 212 AD was very important in the history of civilizations because of the Edict of Caracalla, which made Roman citizens of all individuals living in the Roman Empire. Thanks to this Edict, Hellenism[8] became part of the ruling society; this population was no longer a conquered one, instead they were Roman citizens, that is Romans. Greece had already conquered Rome with its civilization; now Hellenism was politically integral to the rulers of the Empire.[9]

---

[8] Hellenism, as distinguished from the ethnic Greeks, following the teaching of Nicolas Svoronos, as described in: *The Greek Nation, Birth and Shaping of the New Hellenism* (in Greek) (Athens, Polis, 2004). The expansion of the Greek culture in the then known world was performed in two phases. The first was when Alexander the Great brought the Greek culture to the populations which mainly formed the former Persian Empire. The second, when Greece was conquered by and in turn conquered Rome, was because its culture and letters were admired and adopted by the ruling society of the Italian peninsula and around Western Europe. The two expansions had different characteristics, as in the first case the populations adhering to the new culture seem to have lost their cultural independence in relation to the Greeks. Christianity contributed to this. It would nonetheless be a mistake to consider all populations of the late Roman Empire as ethnically Greek; they all shared the same roots in Hellenism, but moved away from this in different ways and with different pace. However, the Latin world never lost its cultural autonomy towards the Greeks.

[9] The attribute 'Roman' has long since lost its ethnic connotation, because of the specific practice of Rome which aimed to extend Roman citizenship to populations beyond the initial boundaries of the city of Rome, and especially to the inhabitants of Italy.

New Rome, Constantinople, and a New Europe

With the conversion of St Paul to Christianity a new chapter of history was opened, because this Jew was also a Roman citizen and educated in Greek. Thanks to him, Christianity became a religion fully reflecting Greek philosophy. Constantine the Great made a move in the same direction and not only adopted Christianity as a new religion of the Empire, but – more than that – he created a new political centre for the Roman Empire, New Rome, called the City of Constantine by the Christian population, also known as Constantinople.

The Emperor Theodosius I had two sons and placed one of them in Rome and one in New Rome; the Empire was not divided into two, the Western and the Eastern Empires, as is commonly portrayed; it was one Empire with two administrations, which was a situation common to the Romans both before and afterwards. After all, there were always two Emperors in the Roman Empire of Constantinople, an echo, perhaps, of the times of two Consuls.

When the barbarian Odoacer killed Romulus Augustulus in 476 AD and took the signals of imperial dignity of the Emperor in Rome, he sent them to the only remaining Emperor of New Rome, Constantinople, and asked for permission to rule Italy in the singular name of the Roman Empire, headed by the Emperor of New Rome. Constantinople accepted the proposal and made him Patrician of the Roman Empire.[10]

Thus Constantinople entered into a new era, trying to govern the lost territories in the name of the Roman Empire through barbarian rulers of all types.[11] In this way, the Roman Emperor of Constantinople acquired, through the dynasties and political realities of the West that he could no longer directly control, the role of supreme representative of international legality, useful to every barbarian who

---

[10] There are many accounts of the early years, when the two administrations of Empire merge into the only one of Constantinople; see C Morrisson (ed), *Le Monde Byzantin, vol I, L'Empire romain d'orient* (Paris, PUF, 2004) 330–641 and especially the contribution by C Morrisson on the continuation of the Roman Empire in the Orient. See also EA Thompson, *Romans and Barbarians: The Decline of the Western Empire* (London / Madison, University of Wisconsin Press, 1982) 61 and J O'Neill, *Holy Warriors: Islam and the Demise of Classical Civilization* (Felibri Publications, 2009) 25.

[11] The case of the Barbarian leader Ataulf is very characteristic, as reported by ancient sources cited in modern bibliography. Henri Pirenne, in his book *Mohammed and Charlemagne* (New York, Meridian Books, 1959), tells the following story at 25–26: '[Ataulf] was determined at all cost to obtain a Roman title. Having quarreled with Jovinus, who was killed in 413, and dismissed Honorius, who remained immovable, he married the beautiful Placidia at Norbonne in 414, which made him the Emperor's brother in law. It is then that he is said to have made the famous declaration recorded by Orosius. "To begin with I ardently desired to efface the very name of the Romans and to transform the Roman Empire into a Gothic Empire. *Romania,* as it is vulgarly called, would have become *Gothia.* Ataulf would have replaced Ceasar Augustus. But long experience taught me that the unruly barbarism of the Goths was incompatible with the laws. Now, without laws there is no state (respublica). I therefore decided rather to aspire to the glory of restoring the fame of Rome in all its integrity and of increasing it by means of the Gothic strength. I hope to go down to posterity as the restorer of Rome since it is not possible that I should be its supplanter"'.

wanted to consolidate his power upon the glory of Rome.[12] At the same time, the Emperor did not abandon his rights of direct sovereignty over the lost territories. Given the opportunity, he tried, throughout the millennium that followed, to re-conquer the lost territories and did not permanently lose southern Italy until the eleventh century (through the abandonment of Bari to the Normans in 1071). During all those years Constantinople and the Roman Emperor were the source of international legality.[13, 14]

The Greco–Roman civilization and letters never disappeared from Europe or the lost territories.[15] It has traditionally been taught that Aristotle was made known to Europeans through the Arabs. However, although Aristotle and a major part of Greek philosophy were adopted by the Arabs, Aristotle and the Greek let-ters never disappeared from Greek education in the Roman Empire. Nor, thanks to Constantinople did they disappear in the West.[16] Christianity played an impor-tant role in this process.[17]

The New Religion, the Roman Empire and Europe

Christianity brought new realities into the ancient world. Unlike other ancient religions, Christianity produced a well-organized clergy, having Christ as its head and a series of dignitaries in an extensive, hierarchical line of servants of the Church. The Church itself was considered to be a congregation of individuals, each of whom had a direct and personal relationship with the founder of the Church, Jesus Christ, who was perceived to be human and God at the same time. However a powerful clergy, claiming to be the direct descendants, in terms of

[12] For the diplomacy of the late Roman Empire, see, among many studies, D Obolensky, 'The Principles and Methods of Byzantine Diplomacy' in *Byzantium and the Slavs* (Yonkers/Crestwood, New York, St Vladimir's Seminary Press, 1994).

[13] There are many studies detailing these issues, among them, see J Herrin, *Byzantium, The Surprising Life of a Medieval Empire* (London, Penguin, 2007); M Angold, *The Byzantine Empire 1025–1204, A Political History*, 2nd edn (London, Longman, 1997).

[14] The best proof of this is the unprecedented account of the peoples, dynasties and relations throughout Europe and beyond, made by the Emperor Constantine VII Porphyrogenitus, in his book, *De Administrando Imperio*, written in Greek under the title Προς τον ίδιον υιόν Ρωμανόν, in the 10th century, a *Commentary* on which is edited by RJH Jenkins, F Dvornik, B Lewis, G Moravcsik, D Obolensky, S Runciman (Dumbarton Oaks Texts, 2012). This book constitutes the proof par excel-lence that the world was living under the glory of Constantinople and the Roman Empire.

[15] See the excellent book by S Gouguenheim, *Aristote au Mont Saint-Michel, les racines grecques de l'Europe chrétienne* (Paris, Seuil, 2008), which successfully modernizes our knowledge on this issue.

[16] Constantinople was a multi-ethnic city with representatives of nations and cultures living or visit-ing the city of the Roman glory and Christian civilization.

[17] JMH Smith, *Europe after Rome, A New Cultural History 500–1000* (Oxford, Oxford University Press, 2005); J Le Goff, *L'Europe est-elle née au Moyen Age?* (Paris, Seuil, 2003).

religious power, of the Archbishop Christ, was developed all over the Roman Empire with a structure following the structure of the Empire itself.[18]

The Bishop of Rome was recognized by all as the spiritual leader of Christians, because, they said, he was holding the seat of St Peter on whom Jesus had conferred the building of his Church. This recognition was rather the result of Christian political pragmatism, as Rome was in those times the political centre of the Empire. The Bishop of Rome, the Pope, would nevertheless have to accept equality with the bishops of other important Christian centres, especially because the Patriarch of Alexandria was recognized by all as the most ancient one. While the Patriarchate of Jerusalem was the only one which could claim to derive directly from Christ, it should not be forgotten that the first elected Bishop of Jerusalem was Jacob, because he was brother of Jesus Christ.

The creation of New Rome by Constantine the Great produced new political challenges for the pragmatist Christians. Soon, the Bishop of New Rome was upgraded to Patriarch and recognized by the Christian world as an administrative equal to the Bishop of Rome. The Pope's spiritual primacy continued, but this would not add up to meaning more than being respected by the other leaders of a polycentric Christianity. In reality, through being close to the Roman Emperor, the Patriarch of Constantinople acquired a platform of unequalled political importance.

Christians adopted the practice of serving the political power of the day and being rewarded by it in exchange. This was perhaps an adaptation of the ancient tradition of having *Pontifex Maximus* as one of the public officials of Rome. In any case, in a society where individuals took the salvation of their souls very seriously, the power of an uncontrolled Church would frighten any Emperor.

Christianity absorbed the ancient culture but reinterpreted it from its own point of view. Since its early triumphant days in the fourth century AD, the Church produced great personalities which, having studied the ancient wisdom, imposed the idea that the inherited culture was to be maintained in the new era, although studied from the point of view of the new truth. Three bishops, St Basil of Caesarea, St Gregory, Patriarch of Constantinople and St John Chrysostom, Patriarch of Constantinople, promoted this idea and its influence continues to be felt today in the Orthodox Church and beyond, as these three are regarded as the protectors of the letters and wisdom.[19]

---

[18] As Peter Brown said in *Power and Persuasion in Late Antiquity: Towards a Christian Empire* (Madison WI, University of Wisconsin Press, 1992) 77, 'With the bishop, the voice of a newly formed urban grouping, the local Christian congregation, came to be heard in the politics of the empire'.

[19] St Basil of Caesarea (329–79), St Gregory Nazianzus (329–90) and St John Chrysostom (347–407), are considered by both Orthodox and Catholic Churches as the Three Holy Hierarchs and Doctors of the Church. The first two were childhood friends from Cappadocia and were educated in rhetoric, law and philosophy, in Constantinople, Antioch, Alexandria and, for six years in Athens (where they studied together with the later Emperor Julian the Apostate). They are known for having brought Hellenism into Christianity and having promoted the study of this ancient wisdom in the new era. St Basil wrote a famous study especially for the youth, delineating how they would be educated though Greek literature, *Address to Young Men on How they Might Derive Benefit from Greek Literature* (Πρὸς τοὺς νέους, ὅπως ἂν ἐξ ἑλληνικῶν ὠφελοῖντο λόγων), ER Maloney, *St Basil the Great to students on Greek literature*,

Although the Church played that important role in preserving ancient knowledge in the new era, it was the Empire's work to educate and not that of the Church.[20] This is very important to stress because the opposite was, or is, considered to have been the case in the western, 'lost' territories of the Roman Empire, which were subsequently ruled by the descendants of the barbarians. The Roman Emperor Theodosius II founded in the early days of 425 AD the University of Constantinople.[21] It was called *Pandidakterion* (a translation to Latin would be *Universitas Studiorum*) and it existed in one form or another up to the fall of the city to the Ottomans, while schools of higher education excelled in Antioch, Beirut, Alexandria and elsewhere.[22] With its vacillating fortunes throughout the centuries, the University of Constantinople effectively promoted knowledge and great scholars, many of whom are still recognized world-wide. In a cosmopolitan city like Constantinople there must have been many coming from Western Europe who took advantage of its educative opportunities.[23]

Law was taught in Constantinople but also in the famous Law School of Antioch as well as elsewhere over the vast Empire. It has been suggested that there was even a connection between the *glossae* of Bologna and those of Constantinople and Beirut.[24]

Moreover, the rapid expansion of Islam through the Arab conquest of many eastern territories of the Roman Empire, and especially Mesopotamia, Syria and Egypt, from the seventh century, was significant because it brought important scholars and well-educated Christian populations to the West. Italy was first to receive them, a place where the Roman Empire was still very influential, but they also migrated to Spain, France, Germany and elsewhere.[25] After all, it needs to be borne in mind that Greek references were endemic in Irish Christianity and that this influenced the British Isles and beyond.

with notes and vocabulary (New York, American Book Company, 1901); NG Wilson, *St Basil on the Value of Greek Literature* (London, Duckworth, 1975); M Naldini (ed), *Basilio di Cesarea: Discorso ai giovani* (Oratio ad Adolescentes, Biblioteca patristica) 3, with the Latin version of Leonardo Bruni (Florence, Nardini, 1984).

[20] See an excellent account of the years of transition in the 6th and 7th centuries, in: Morrisson, *Le Monde Byzantin*, above n 10, and especially on education by B Flusin.

[21] The closing of a Neo-Platonist Academy in Athens by Justinian I in 529 AD has become a symbol of the idea that Christianity brought the world into barbarism. The original Academy had survived until 83 BC and then re-established as a Neo-Platonist school of thought in 410 AD. Whatever the importance of that decision might have been, it needs to be remembered that there were many schools around the Empire and the University of Constantinople, and, therefore, the letters never ceased to be studied and advanced, not only from a theological point of view in the monasteries, but – most importantly – as a product of society and for society.

[22] Among others, see Herrin, *Byzantium*, above n 13 at 240.

[23] Constantinople was the biggest city in Christendom and a very cosmopolitan one, Herrin, above n 13 at 461.

[24] On this issue, see among others, W Kaiser, 'Berytos and Bologna, Some Remarks on Fritz Pringsheim' in Flogaitis and Pantelis, *The Eastern Roman Empire and the Birth of the Idea of State in Europe*, above n 1 at 343.

[25] Gouguenheim, *Aristote au Mont Saint-Michel*, above n 15, and further references.

Christianity[26] became, in fact, a tool to aid the absorption of the new comers in Europe[27] – the so-called 'barbarian' tribes – into a culturally homogenized Europe.[28] Through the Christian religion and the power of faith, all the systems of values, in tandem with the principles of political organization, rapidly expanded throughout Europe to become a form of common heritage. Terrible warriors who had terrified Europe became the fervent defenders of Christ and, through that, reflected and perpetuated the religion of the Greco–Roman civilization.[29]

Charlemagne, Holy Roman Empire of the German Nation, Constantinople

The international political situation began to change following the dawn of the ninth century, when the new populations of Western Europe began to mature economically, spiritually and politically.[30] This process was largely driven by the huge influence of Constantinople and its culture, the natural source for every other cultural derivative of the time. This maturation brought with it a vision of a new relationship with Roman glory, more locally-based, and with reference to Rome rather than the New Rome.

[26] At this point it needs to be stressed that the role of Christianity in the expansion of the Greco–Roman civilization should not be understood in terms of excluding Judaism from that development. No matter how easy or difficult relations between two religions were through the centuries, Judaism has, without any doubt, been, since ancient times, part of that civilization and has contributed to its expansion through knowledge. Judaic communities were scattered throughout the Roman Empire before the destruction of the Temple, living in a fully integrated way as part of the dominant civilization. Sometimes they were fully Hellenized; this was the case, for example, within the Judaic communities of Alexandria, which had lost their ability to read Hebrew. This led Ptolemeus II to decide upon the translation of the Ancient Testament into Greek. In addition, the Jewish communities, who had always been educated, contributed decisively in introducing the new societies in the West to ancient Greek letters and Aristotle. The key figure of influence here was Maimonides, the Jewish philosopher of Cordoba who wrote in Arabic. His works opened up new ways of understanding the Greco–Roman civilization and, translated into Latin, exercised a wide influence in the West and, in particular, on St Thomas Aquinas. On the other hand, the Greco–Roman civilization inherited by Europe and, beyond it, by the world, was not the pagan civilization of the old times, but a Christian civilization, ie full of Judaic principles and teaching.

[27] There are excellent studies in this area, among many: CM Cusack, *Rise of Christianity in Northern Europe, 300–1000* (London, Bloomsbury, 1998); RA Fletcher, *The Barbarian Conversion: From Paganism to Christianity* (New York, H Holt and Co, 1998).

[28] The struggle of the established Church to fight Arianism was moving in that direction, because that heresy was adopted by the Germans, who were to be influential players in the new Europe.

[29] The expansion of the Greek civilization started, of course, with the conquests of Alexander the Great and continued as expansion of the Greco–Roman civilization with the conquests of the Romans, especially in Western and Northern Europe. Barbarian invasions, however, left that civilization under threat, while there remained vast European territories that had never come under Roman rule. An excellent example of this was the Christianization of the Slavs through which they were brought into European civilization.

[30] TC Lounghis, 'The Formation of European States and their Shifting Diplomatic Relationships with the Eastern Roman Empire 476–1089' in Flogaitis and Pantelis, *The Eastern Roman Empire and the Birth of the Idea of State in Europe*, above n 1 at 159.

Within this political landscape, characterized by the new political significance of the Franks, the Bishop of Rome aspired to create a new political Roman legitimacy for his benefit. This was made possible by crowning Charlemagne Roman Emperor during Christmas of the year 800, thus overlooking the Roman Emperor of Constantinople and – for the first time – making himself a source of imperial legitimacy.

Charlemagne requested, as required by the international order of the times that his title be recognized by Constantinople[31] and eventually decided to settle on the title of Emperor, 'who governs the empire for the Romans, King of the Franks and the Lombards and patrician of the Romans'.[32] The Roman Emperor was also compromising,[33] as he now had definitively to accept a second Christian Emperor on Earth, who would dominate most of the lost territories of the Empire in Western Europe. As part of this struggle of the West for political autonomy from the system of Constantinople, and in order to claim Roman glory as their own, the rulers of the West began to call the Roman Emperor Greek King.

Western Europe, its dynasties and its societies, matured under the radiant influence of Constantinople[34] but they could now dream of devouring their mother.[35] This ideological removal occurred gradually through economic penetration to the East, which was more evident in the eleventh century, when that penetration was matched by a military one. The crusades began during the same period and these constitute a massive exposure and learning process for the Western societies of those times, as the two worlds were forged together.[36] The looting of Constantinople remained very deep in the memories of both worlds but, in truth, the intellectual looting was of a much greater significance to the history of mankind.[37]

Those times also witnessed the foundation of what was later called the Holy Roman Empire of the German Nation, a political formation that would not compromise with Constantinople as did Charlemagne. It claimed both Roman

---

[31] About the immediate reactions of the Roman Empire of Constantinople: *Einhardi Vita Caroli Magni*, c 16, MGH SS, 2, 451 33-452.4 9MGH SRG, pp 19.26–20.8) and c 28; *Theophanes Chronographia*, C de Boor, 1 (Leipzig, 1833) 1, 494 20–25.

[32] P Classen, 'Romanum gubernans imperium: Zum Vorgeschichte der Kaisertitulatur Karls des Grossen' (1952) 9 *Deutsches Archiv fur Erforschung des Mittelalters* 103.

[33] See among others, GD Guyon, 'Questions autour du modèle institutionnel du christianisme: Trait d'union entre l'Orient et l'Occident' in Flogaitis and Pantelis, *The Eastern Roman Empire and the Birth of the Idea of State in Europe*, above n 1 at 91.

[34] See M Kaplan, 'La polulation de Constantinople du VIe siècle à l'époque des Paléologues' in Flogaitis and Pantelis, ibid at 73.

[35] J Le Goff has written an unparalleled study on the civilization of the West also in its crossroads with the civilization of Constantinople, in *La civilisation de l'occident médiéval*, 1st edn 1964 (Arthaud, 1984); also, D Nicholas, *The Evolution of the Medieval World, Society, Government and Thought in Europe, 312–1500* (London, Longman, 1992).

[36] One of the excellent examples of this is the history of the Inner Temple, London.

[37] For an excellent study of the medieval political thought, see JH Burns (ed), *The Cambridge History of Medieval Political Thought, c 350–c 1450*, 2nd edn (Cambridge, Cambridge University Press, 2010); also, A Black, *Political Thought in Europe, 1250–1450*, 2nd edn (Cambridge Medieval Textbooks, Cambridge University Press, 2000).

heritage and the title of the Empire, while it recorded – for the first time – the desire of the German Nation to be registered as the inheritor of the shining tradition.[38]

This Empire, that was, in substance, no more than a quaint, loose confederation of kings and princes (especially of the German territories and those of German influence) was created in 962 AD when the Bavarian King Otto I was crowned Emperor by the Pope. In this way, Otto I acquired the legitimacy to succeed Charlemagne, in accordance with the theories promoted by the papacy. His son, Otto II, proclaimed himself Emperor of the Romans (*Imperator Romanorum*) – a title which Constantinople never recognized – and, in order to symbolize this, was offered Theophany as a wife. She was a woman who came from an imperial family but one of secondary political importance. Unfortunately for Constantinople, Otto II died suddenly. Subsequently, this Empire added the adjective 'Holy' and later that of 'of the German Nation'.

This political assertion produced two significant pivotal features: first, the definitive schism of the Churches in 1054, which was due to the Pope's desire to convert his spiritual primacy into administrative primacy, aiming at reviving Rome towards Constantinople. Second was the fall of Constantinople to the Crusaders in 1204, when the armies of Western Europe took the title of Roman Emperor, undervalued it politically in order to serve the new significance of their nations, and gave it to Frankish princes of minor political importance.

Of course, historical developments in this region of the world have not always been linear. Thus, 60 years later, Constantinople drove out the invaders and the Roman Empire survived for a further 200 years. The Empire of Constantinople would nevertheless be continuously held to account for its Roman character, for its role in the world, and ultimately for its value. The West would continue developing in an upward direction and would increasingly demonstrate great cruelty towards Constantinople. The Empire would continuously be accused of being a cradle of intrigues, corruption, moral decadence and so on, a city ignoring current truths now represented by the new powers and societies of the West. According to them, that Empire could no longer claim the right to be called Roman; it was just Greek, headed by a Greek Basileus. It seems that the only ones at that time who recognized the Roman character of the Empire were the Ottomans, perhaps because they wanted, in their turn, to be the successors of a glorious Roman past. Even today, they call the Greeks of their territory Romans (*Roum*).[39]

---

[38] Paul Magdalino gives an excellent description of the power antagonisms among the Emperor, the Pope and the German rulers, especially F Barbarossa, in: *The Empire of Manuel I Komnenos, 1143–80* (Cambridge, Cambridge University Press, 1993) especially 83–109.

[39] *Romios* (Roman), as a form of nomenclature for the Greeks, was widespread up to modern times although it is used to a lesser extent nowadays. In the times of the Greek Revolution there was discussion about how they should refer to themselves, because they had lived for centuries under different names, such as *Romios, Graikos* or *Ellinas*. They chose the words *Ellinas* and *Ellas*, instead of the foreign translations deriving of the Latin Greek and Greece. However, the term *Romios* for Greek and *Romiosyni* for Greece have always been utilized as alternatives in society and everyday life.

The Late Roman Empire and the Concept of State

Unlike the classic Roman Empire, the late Roman Empire had a well-developed administration.[40] There was a system of ministers[41] with various individuals surrounding the Emperor, and an administration from Constantinople whose influence was felt in the most remote provinces of the Empire.[42] Taking into consideration the times, this administration was meticulously organized, both professionally and hierarchically. It had a regional organizational structure called *Themata*, under the command of a *Stratigos*.

Aside from the ordinary business of any administration, the purpose of this administration was to collect the taxes. Alongside it was a system of judges, providing justice to the people in the name of the Emperor.[43]

Following the old Roman principle, there were two separate treasuries, the public treasury of the Empire (the *Aerarium*, to which the *Fiscus* was added during the imperial era) and the second which belonged personally to the Emperor (*patrimonium, res privata*).

The Roman Empire was governed by public law, a system of rules imposed upon everyone by the sole will of the Emperor.

---

[40] 'The omnipotence of the emperor and the transformation of the state into a bureaucracy now realized their full development', G Ostrogorsky, *History of the Byzantine State* (J Hassey tr, Oxford, Blackwell, 1980) 245.

[41] Giannini writes: 'Even Byzantium, which as they say "invented" the ministries, in reality it only introduced the ministers, as offices-organs helping the Crown, in other words it stabilizes and gives a name to offices which existed already as internal offices of the Emperor', in *Il potere pubblico*, above n 2 at 27–28. It is true that those officials had all sorts of names, many of them misleading indicators of their true powers. However, it is equally true that ongoing research proves the opposite, especially because there was a well-developed public administration across the entire Empire.

[42] Most interestingly, there was a fully developed system of ceremonies. The best-known description of imperial life in Constantinople was produced by an Emperor, Constantine VII Porphyrogenitus (913–59 AD) in his *Book of Ceremonies*. See among many, A Cameron, D Cannadine and SRF Price, *The Construction of Court Ritual: The Byzantine Book of Ceremonies* (Cambridge, Cambridge University Press, 1987) 106 and AJ Toynbee, *Constantine Porphyrogenitus and his World* (Oxford, Oxford University Press, 1973) 575–605. A similar book was published in the 14th century under the name of *George Codinos* (J Verpeaux (ed), *Pseudo-Codinos, Traité des offices* (Paris, Editions du Centre national de la recherche scientifique, 1906/1966)). The imperial ceremonies had impressed the Western World, as is proven through the descriptions of Bishop Liutprand of Cremona, who visited Constantinople twice in 949 AD and 968 AD and extensively describes some of them in his reports. Among many, see Cameron, Cannadine and Price, *The Construction of Court Ritual*, ibid 119. What relationship there is, if any, between the ceremonies of the Empire of Constantinople and those adopted and developed in the courts of the rest of Europe, needs further research.

[43] N Svoronos, 'Le serment de fidélité à l'empereur byzantin et sa signification constitutionnelle' (1951) 9 *Revue des Etudes Byzantines* 106; LA Neville, 'Imperial Administration and Byzantine Political Culture' in *Authority in Byzantine Provincial Society, 950–1100* (Cambridge, Cambridge University Press, 2004); JB Bury, *The Imperial Administrative System of the Ninth Century, with a Revised Text of the Kletorologion of Philotheos* (Oxford, Oxford University Press, 1911); H Saradi, 'The Byzantine Tribunals: Problems in the Application of Justice and State Policy' (1995) 53 *Revue des Etudes Byzantines* 195.

The Emperor was not hereditary, but elected, the process for which followed rules which changed over the centuries. Theoretically he was elected[44] and practically, he was appointed by acclamation of the army, but after that – in order to acquire popular investiture – he had to present himself to the Senate and then to the people in the hippodrome of Constantinople.[45] The Senate, the people, and the army were the three constitutional elements of the Empire till the end.[46] He was crowned in St Sophia, the biggest and most renowned church on Earth, as he was the representative of God on Earth.[47] However, in essence, his power did not come from God,[48] but from the army, the Senate and the people, the three constitutional elements of the Empire.[49] Finally, he obtained a personal oath, from all the three constitutional elements of the Empire, plus from the Church

[44] 'The principle of elective Monarchy persisted in theory all along the byzantine era, but in reality only a few emperors came to power after elections, the institution of the co-emperor being the combination between the principle of the elective Monarchy and the hereditary Monarchy ... The concept of the divine source of the imperial power is already present in the fifth century. The imperial power becomes independent and ceases deriving from the electors of the emperor. The importance of the Senate, the army and the people, constitutional elements of the empire, starts diminishing considerably' N Svoronos, 'Le serment de fidélité à l'Empereur Byzantin et sa signification constitutionnelle' (1951) 9 *Revue des Etudes Byzantines* 116–17.

[45] 'The same sense of continuous development is suggested by another prominent feature of the Byzantine rituals, namely their constant use of formulaic acclamation. It may seem surprising to read, in the Book of ceremonies, that on religious as well secular occasions, the lengthy acclamations of the emperors were performed by choirs of the Blues and the Greens, the old circus factions'. Cameron, Cannadine and Price, *The Construction of Court Ritual*, above n 42 at 127. Also, HG Beck, *Senat und Volk von Konstantinopel, Probleme der byzantinischen Verfassungsgeschichte – Sitzungsberichte* (Bayerische Akademie der Wissenschaften, philosoph.-hist. Klasse. München, 1967/1966); MV Anastos, '*Vox Populi Voluntas Dei* and the Election of the Byzantine Emperor' in *Studies in Judaism and Late Antiquity, 12, Christianity, Judaism and other Greco–Roman Cults*, 2 (Leiden, EJ Brill, 1975) 181–207.

[46] Svoronos, 'Le serment de fidélité à l'Empereur Byzantin et sa signification constitutionnelle', above n 44 at 125.

[47] In fact, before Christianity was imposed as the religion of the Empire, the Emperor was considered as God. In the new reality, he had to abandon his claim to divinity and became, instead, the defender of the faith, by being the representative of God on Earth.

[48] On this issue Nicolas Svoronos discusses the position of other byzantinists, according to whom the Patriarch crowned the Emperor because he was the first citizen of the Empire. He writes: 'I believe that there is no doubt that the fact that the Patriarch crowns the Emperor constitutes a purely religious act, and the Patriarch does not act as the first citizen but in his quality as priest and chief of the religion ...Those are above all purely religious acts, which demonstrate without any doubt, the importance that religion starts acquiring in Byzantium. But I do not believe that we should see the Church as a fourth constitutional element of the Empire', above n 44 at 126. An excellent account of the sources of power in the Roman Empire of Constantinople is in W Ensslin, 'Zur Frage nach der ersten Kaiserkrönung durch den Patriarchen und zur Bedeutung dieses Aktes im Wahlzeremoniell' (1942) 42 *Byzantinische Zeitschrift* 101; and *Gottkaiser und Kaiser von Gottes Gnaden* (Bayerische Akademie der Wissenschaften, phil.-hist. Klasse. Sitzungsberichte, 1943) 6; also, R Guilland, 'Le Droit divin à Byzance' in *Études Byzantines* (Paris, 1959) 207; D Feissel, *La pétition à Byzance*, Centre de Recherche d'Histoire et Civilisation de Byzance, Monographies 14 (Paris, Association des Amis du Centre d'Histoire et Civilisation de Byzance, 2004).

[49] For an excellent account of the transition from the institutions of the Imperial Roman Empire to those of the late Roman Empire, in particular, those taking place in the times of Emperor Heraclius in the 7th century, see Morrisson, *Le Monde Byzantin*, above n 10, and especially the contribution of D Feissel on the Emperor and the imperial administration.

through the Patriarch.[50] A detailed record of those oaths was kept in the imperial archives; the oath should be renewed every time that a new Emperor came to power.[51]

The Emperor could equally be either male or female, and several females became Emperors throughout the centuries. The most famous, perhaps, was Irina, who was on the throne of Constantinople when Charlemagne was crowned by the Pope as Roman Emperor. It seems that the Pope eluded to Charlemagne that the Roman throne was empty because it was held by a woman. The Emperor usually appointed a second Emperor to help him and eventually replace him during times of war campaigns; in this way, several Emperors imposed their sons as their successors to the throne; they did so by crowning them themselves, immediately after their own coronations.

Crucially, however, the late Roman Empire did not experience feudalism.[52] Feudalism was a way of organizing the society which had nothing to do with the Roman tradition of societal organization. It could be seen as its antithesis, a structure without either public or state powers.

Feudalism relied on a system of interpersonal relations, with a hierarchy of individuals where each one of them had sworn submission and loyalty to his immediate superior, the submission to the king or prince being only indirect in most cases. This submission meant that the sworn-in should offer his services in peace and at war to his superior along with an annually-versed percentage of his agricultural production. In return for this submission, the superior should offer his protection on all occasions and in multifarious ways.

This system did not encompass or reflect the distinction between private law and public law, it belonged to what was known as *common law*; it was practically a feature of private law, in our way of understanding law, because it was the private business of free men. In fact, apart from those who had constituted this network of individuals, all other individuals, mainly peasants, belonged more or less to the

---

[50] Meaning that the Patriarch, after having crowned the Emperor, declared his submission both for himself as well as as representative of the Church.

[51] This oath, after the cross-fertilization which was produced during the crusades with Western customs of similar character but of feudal origin, has generated debate among both contemporaries and modern historians.

[52] On this issue, see generally, A Laiou (ed), *The Economic History of Byzantium from the Seventh through the Fifteenth Century* (Washington DC, Dumbarton Oaks Research Library and Collection, 2002), A Harvey, *Economic Expansion in the Byzantine Empire, 900–1200*, 1st edn (Cambridge, Cambridge University Press, 1989). Among the first approaches of the issue of feudalism in the late Roman Empire was the one proposed by G Ostrogorsky, *Pour l'histoire de la féodalité byzantine* (Brussels, Editions de l'Institut de Philologie et d'Histoire Orientales et Slaves, 1954). That study opened the discussion to other historians who developed a different approach, especially the one of N Svoronos, 'Société et organization intérieure dans l'empire byzantin au XIIe siècle: les principaux problèmes' in *Proceedings of the XIIIth International Congress of the Byzantine Studies, Oxford 1966* (London, 1967) 384–89, and 'Remarques sur les structures économiques de l'empire byzantin au XIe siècle' (1976) 6 *Travaux et Mémoires* 62–3. See also, P Lemerle, *The Agrarian History of Byzantium from the Origins to the Twelfth Century: The Sources and Problems* (Galway, Galway University Press, 1979) and *Cinq etudes sur le XIe siècle byzantin* (Paris, Editions du Centre national de la recherche scientifique, 1977).

land they had the chance to cultivate, both for their own living and for the system they were serving.

Feudalism was mainly a system of organizing society on the basis of agricultural production; however, it also produced a system of government.

Agricultural production cannot, however, provide the basis for any more sophisticated societal system, because, ultimately, a society needs lawyers, doctors, pharmacies, banks, and a plethora of other services. Moreover, there were groups within the population who were deprived of the possibility of having land of their own, others who did not have any religious-rooted issue with lending money with interest, and others who were ready to travel in order to make fortunes through commerce, others who favoured education or religious affairs, and so on. Those people constituted the cities and towns of the feudal system, or the monasteries – all necessary additions to the agricultural societies of the time. As they were useful to the system, they were able to negotiate and acquire freedoms and special regimes. These were the origins of what was later called decentralization in France; at the same time the cities were to produce political and financial changes which would bring the societies beyond feudalism.

English feudalism, as established by William the Conqueror,[53] had specific characteristics, which produced different results. In England, members of the feudal hierarchy at every level had to be sworn in directly to the King.[54] Therefore, every feudal, independent of his rank, was accountable directly to the King and not to his immediate superior. This was also the case with the boroughs, which became, through this, cities–organs of the Crown. These were the origins of what was later called self-government in England.[55]

---

[53] The debate historians, economists, philosophers and lawyers, have about the introduction of feudalism in England as one of the consequences of the Norman Conquest, its significance and peculiarities, is very rich. See, among many, M Chibnall, *The Debate on the Norman Conquest* (New York, Manchester University Press, 1999). The discussion goes back to the 17th century, eg J Cowell, *Institutiones iuris anglicani, ad methodum et seriem institutionum imperialium compositae et digestae* (Oxoniae, Oxlad ua, 1676); W Fulbecke, *A Parallele or Conference of the Civill Law, the Canon Law, and the Common Law of this Realme of England. Where in the agreement and disagreement of these three Lawes . . . are opened and discussed [etc]* (London, printed by Thomas Wight, 1601). In modern times, see JGA Pocock, *The Ancient Constitution and the Feudal Law. A Study of English Historical Thought in the Seventeenth Century*, 1st edn (Cambridge, University Press, 1957); C Wickham, 'The Other Transition: From the Ancient World to Feudalism' (1984) 103 *Past and Present* 3; EAR Brown, 'The Tyranny of a Construct: Feudalism and Historians of Medieval Europe' (1974) 79 *American Historical Review* 1063; S Reynolds, *Fiefs and Vassals: The Medieval Evidence Reinterpreted* (New York and Oxford, Oxford University Press, 1994).

[54] Reminding us of such an interesting echoing of features the legal constitutional order of the Empire of Constantinople with the oath that everyone had to give personally and individually to the King. Later, Henry VIII introduced a system of relations with the Church where the Church had to submit to the King, in a similar way to that earlier practice in Constantinople.

[55] S Flogaitis, *Administrative Law et droit administratif* (Paris, Pichon et Durand-Auzias, 1986).

Concluding Remarks

The development of public powers began to enjoy resurgence in Europe from the middle of the fourteenth century, and gradually replaced the institutions of feudalism in favour of the creation of states.[56] This is typically understood to have been achieved by coincidence as the result of addressing new needs with *ad hoc* answers provided by feudal dignitaries with the help of lawyers.

History teaches, however, that institutions do not develop by coincidence but principally through the inherited ideas of more advanced or experienced civilizations.[57] Thanks to recent ongoing studies of the late Roman Empire, it also appears that Europe was reshaped on the matrix offered by that Empire. This preserved its knowledge, developed the public structures inherited by the classic Roman Empire, took lessons from organizational structures of older civilizations of the East and amalgamated them with the Roman tradition.[58] Most importantly, it

---

[56] P Stein, *Roman Law in European History* (Cambridge, Cambridge University Press, 1999).

[57] Unfortunately for the history of civilizations, Byzantium still suffers today from misconceptions advanced by the philosophy of the Lights and – for the English-speaking world in particular – by Gibbon's ideas perhaps having their roots in the times of Liutprand. Cameron wrote: 'Gibbon's *Decline and Fall* has a lot to answer for in this regard, and old ideas (however inappropriate to a different age) die hard. They start from a too-ready assumption that a highly stratified bureaucracy and a highly codified elite structure indicate a generally static or immobile society', in *The Construction of Court Ritual*, above n 42 at 132.

[58] One of the most interesting, if not intriguing, questions for historians of institutions, is the relation between Constantinople and the British Isles and possible influences on the emerging English society and state structure. On this issue, see S Laws, 'Contacts between the Eastern Roman Empire and Anglo-Saxon England' in Flogaitis and Pantelis, *The Eastern Roman Empire and the Birth of the Idea of State in Europe*, above n 1 at 217. It is well-established that Christianity came to Britain from Ireland and that it was full of Greek references, while in 668 a Greek from Tarsus called Theodore was appointed Archbishop of Canterbury, the very first to be buried in the cathedral. It is also known that, in the 8th and 9th centuries, Greek monks came to England because of the policies against the icons in the Roman Empire, bringing their culture to the isles; also Englishmen – one of whom was also the secretary to William the Conqueror – participated in a German bishop's pilgrimage in 1064. The chronicles of the times also detail that the last Anglo-Saxon King had sent a delegation to the Roman Empire, because of a dream which had emotionally upset him. On the other hand, the diplomatic and cultural relations between the two worlds never ceased. It should be noted that when England was taken by the Normans, according to the English chronicles of the times, 350 or 235 ships – the exact number varies according to different chronicles – full of Anglo-Saxons (reportedly about 30,000), left the country and sailed to Constantinople seeking protection, and that they gave rise to the transformation of the Varangian Imperial Guard into the English Imperial Guard. They were the so-called 'Oriental Angli' and served the Emperor until the end of the Empire. Most significantly, there are reports of several diplomatic and other envoys in both directions and Emperor Manuel Comnenos, proposed to King Henry II in 1170 that his daughter should be married to his son, a project which never materialized. In his letter the Emperor was reminding the King that his children from his second wife, Mary of Antioch, were second cousins to the King's children from his wife Queen Eleanor. The embassy came from Constantinople to London in 1176 and was reciprocated by the visit of an English Knight, Geoffrey de Haie, to Constantinople. The visit of Emperor Manuel II Paleologos to King Henry IV for two months during Christmas of 1400 at the palace of Eltham was but one example of intensified relations between the two worlds in those days. Strangely, the general received opinion in modern England is that the two worlds were very remote from each other and that cross-fertilization was thus impossible, until the revival of the Greek letters centuries later. Further historical research into this special relationship between the

made them known to the world, through education, political influence, and the spread of Roman glory to emergent societies.

two worlds which brought the Anglo-Saxons to the service of the Emperor and the Emperor to London, is needed. This is because it could help illuminate and explain aspects of the birth and evolution of core characteristics of English society and its institutions. On the general issue of the relations between Byzantium and England, see the excellent study by Donald M Nicol, *Studies in Late Byzantine History and Prosopography* (London, Variorum Reprints, 1986) and, in particular, the chapter entitled 'Byzantium and England', 157, where further bibliography is cited, with references to ancient chronicles.

Lesson 2

Public Administration

The development of a public administration – defined as a system of individuals and means hierarchically organized in a pyramid from the centre to the periphery of a given political organization – as we have already mentioned, is commonly accepted as the central characteristic around which the concept of state was conceived and modern states were instituted.[1] At this point, it is therefore important further to elaborate on what we mean by the term 'public administration' and its regime. We also need to examine all areas aside from the state, which have developed well-organized administrative systems in modern times. The starting point for this was the concept of *jus politiae*.

Jus Politiae

Towards the end of feudal times and especially during the fourteenth century, French lawyers proposed the term 'police' from the Greek term '$\pi o\lambda\iota\tau\epsilon\iota\alpha$'; it was intended to capture the sense of the rulemaking power of the Prince,[2] a secular authority. This meant that the Prince, or the state, was reserving and differentiating for itself a role and ultimate aims which were different from those of the Church, which was the pre-existing authority.

This defined the *jus politiae*, which gradually became the cradle of power of the Prince and the state.[3] It was understood as the right and duty of the Prince to exercise the necessary powers over his territory's subjects in order to satisfy the need for public order and welfare. In this way, state and police developed in parallel and in strict interdependence, with the result that every new area of public authority was seen as being part of the police, the *jus politiae*. The development of the

---

[1] MS Giannini, *Il pubblico potere, Stati e amministrazioni pubbliche* (Bologna, Il Mulino, 1986) 28ff; E Forsthoff, *Verfassungsgeschichte der Neuzeit* (Stuttgart, Kohlhammer, 1961).

[2] S Flogaitis, *Les contrats administratifs* (London, Esperia, 1998) 62ff; J-L Martres, *Caractères généraux de la police économique* (Bordeaux, Thèse, 1964); E Picard, *La notion de police administrative* (Paris, LGDJ, 1984); E Forsthoff, ibid.

[3] O Mayer, *Le droit administratif allemand*, vol I (Paris, Giard et Brière, 1903) 30ff; M Stolleis, *Geschichte des öffentlichen Rechts in Deutschland*, vol I (München, Beck, 2012) 369; P Preu, *Polizeibegriff und Staatszwecklehre, Die Entwicklung Polizeibegriffs durch die Rechts- und Staatswissenschaften des 10. Jahrhunderts* (Göttingen, Vanderhök und Ruprecht, 1983).

powers of the state necessarily required the development of state competencies which took shape through the conceptual and literal development of the police.

The concept of *jus politiae* migrated from France to Germany during the fifteenth century and developed further in the two subsequent centuries. It was understood as a principle which gave the Prince the right and duty to impose public order (*gute Ordnung*) on his territory. It became known as '*Policey*', '*Poletzey*', '*Pollucy*', '*Pollicei*' and was always underscored by notions of public order (*gute Ordnung*), good government (*gutes Regiment*), security (*Sicherheit*), public interest (*gemein Nutzen*) and assistance by the public authorities. Gradually the definition of the term grew to encompass everything which the state, with its right to act unilaterally, could do for the general welfare of the people (*gemeine Wohlfahrt*). Otto Mayer wrote that there could be no possible limits to the right to exercise '*police*'.[4]

According to the German lawyers, the *jus politiae* gave the sovereign the right to take all possible measures to realize happiness on Earth (*irdische Glückseligkeit*) for their subjects.[5] Through this means of justification, it gave the political power the possibility to impose itself on all private activities and thus became the basis of the absolute power of the state. The '*Etat policier*' or '*Polizeistaat*' ceded its place to the absolutist state. Police (*Policey*) and state government became one and the same.[6]

That *jus politiae*, after having given rise to the so-called *Polizeistaat*, evolved into what modern French public law terms '*pouvoirs régaliens*'. By this I mean the competencies of the state, which have traditionally been considered the expression par excellence of state sovereignty as, for example, the protection of public order, the currency, the control of foreign commerce and of rulemaking power. Each of these form part of a collection of competences for which French public law never produced a general criterion; in fact, they constitute the core notion of the *jus politiae* of both past and present.[7]

Such competence or jurisdiction is at the centre of all discussion about the state, and it is always a rule, in other words the definition of a competence or jurisdiction is always made by a rule. These concepts form the fundamental core of the *jus politiae* and are always considered as rules of public order.[8]

The most important consequence of the *jus politiae* is that the state *has the duty* to exercise its powers and especially its regulatory powers. Therefore, it cannot bind itself by contract in the exercise of its regulatory powers. A contract between

---

[4] Mayer, *Le droit administratif allemand*, above n 3 at 31, where he adds: 'More and more new things had to be dealt with. Police became because of that a continuous source of new competences that the prince can obtain, the content of which he determines personally, thanks to the *jus politiae*'.

[5] F Fleiner, *Instituzionen des deutschen Verwaltungsrechts* (Tübingen, JCB Mohr (P Siebeck), 1919) 360.

[6] G Poggi, *Lo Stato: natura, sviluppo, prospettive* (Bologna, Il Mulino, 1992) 55 (ch 3, 'Lo sviluppo dello stato moderno').

[7] A de Laubadère et al, *Traité des contrats administratifs*, vol I (Paris, LGDJ, 1983) 47.

[8] As already stated by E Laferrière, *Traité de la juridiction administrative et des recours contentieux*, vol II (Paris, LGDJ, 1989) 117.

the state and anyone else, by which the state promises either to do or not to do something in the future in the area of its rulemaking power is not binding for the state and of no effect. However, the state might be responsible for the payment of damages for its illegal behaviour.[9]

The eighteenth century was the era in which states created powerful administrative structures. In those years France was no longer – as it had previously been – the model of the evolution. In its place were the central European powers, Austria, the German States, and Italian States, evolving under central European influence. The eighteenth century witnessed the inception and development of the so-called absolutist state.

The major characteristic feature of these times was that many very distinguished philosophers focused upon both concept and realities of the state. Some took on important political positions and so had the opportunity to realize political visions for the state.

Under these new influences, the tradition of the *jus politiae* emphatically made its mark on the new concept of state: everybody became convinced that the state had the welfare of its subjects as its primary aim; the political philosophers of the time referred to this as Welfare State (*Wohlfahrtsstaat*). This concept ushered into the political philosophy the idea that the state exists in order to meet interests that it adopts for its own, in other words, public interests. Wherever the state concluded that it had obligation to adopt an interest, that interest would become public interest.

In this way, the states developed all sorts of policies during the eighteenth century, intervening in almost every aspect of societal activity. They built theatres, opera houses, and cultural centres of all sorts, in addition to hospitals, markets, schools, and universities. They regulated agriculture, they created state-owned industries, especially for the needs of the army, and so on. Never before had so many activities been initiated or generated by the public powers.[10]

Behind this philosophy it is often possible to see the influences of the *bourgeoisie* in an interesting confluence with those of representatives of the aristocracy. But it was true that Europe had not seen so many philosophers interested in the questions of society, public power, and the state for centuries. Of this collection of philosophers, the English occupied the central role.[11]

Many of the ideas developed during those times by these people would come to the fore in the next era, one which started with the great American Revolution of 1787 and continued with the great French Revolution of 1789. Baron de Montesquieu was the most famous among them, as was the book *De l'esprit des lois*.

The result of such developments was that everywhere in the countries with absolutist states – and especially in those of the so-called states of illuminated

---

[9] Flogaitis, *Les contrats administratifs*, above n 2 at 50ff.

[10] Giannini, *Il pubblico potere*, above n 1 at 31ff.

[11] Giannini notes that, unlike the state which emerged from the French Revolution, the absolutist state did not respond to a certain typology and each one of them followed its own path, ibid at 61ff and further citations.

absolutism – public administrations were seen as the machinery of the Crown. This potent legacy continues today, as the head of state in modern democracies is also the head of the administration, and head of the executive.

On the other hand, the same conclusions could also be drawn for the states with 'democratic' government, as, for example, the Netherlands of those times. This observation could, perhaps, lead to the conclusion that such developments were the result of their historical context rather than the specific form of state.[12]

Everything soon changed, however, thanks to the development of the British parliamentary system, together with the promulgation of the Constitution of the United States of America, and the French Revolution. Nevertheless, these new realities inherited a strong administration; bureaucracy was a term which appeared in usage at that time in France. Simultaneously balancing both positive and negative meanings, it was meant to be the spine of the newly-articulated states.

Public Administration and Public Law

The right and duty of the Prince to have rulemaking activities to promote the wellbeing of society as part of the *jus politiae*, revived the Roman distinction between private and public law.[13] The Prince could and had to take all decisions which he considered necessary and useful, and those rules could be imposed on private individuals by the sole will of the Prince, what Germans referred to as the *Herrschaft*.

Public law became a very strong tool in the hands of the power because it was the law of unilateral will and of rulemaking which had nothing to do with contract. It has been commonly accepted since Roman times that the contract is the law of the parties stipulating it; by contrast, public law is the law of all who, coupled with this, are ruled without having necessarily been asked for their opinion. For this reason public law particularly developed during the times of the *Polizeistaat* and the absolutist state.

The French Revolution adopted the same principle and public law was meant to be the only legal system governing public administration. After all, it was a time of revolution and every new system needs a powerful arm to help impose its will on society. The Revolution not only followed the tradition of the absolutist state but also required that public law be the law of the state and, in particular, of public administration.[14]

---

[12] Giannini, ibid.

[13] For the revival of Roman law in the European states, see P Stein, *Roman Law in European History* (Cambridge, Cambridge University Press, 1999) 71ff.

[14] See, among others, G Bigot, *Introduction historique au droit administratif depuis 1789* (Paris, Presses Universitaires de France, 2002); F Burdeau, *Histoire du droit administratif* (Paris, Presses Universitaires de France, 1995); J-L Mestre, *Introduction historique au droit administratif français* (Paris, Presses Universitaires de France, 1985).

In order to secure that principle, the Revolution entirely excluded the public administration from control by the judiciary; the public administration would be the sole judge of its activity, achieved in the name of a specific interpretation of the principle of the separation of powers.[15]

The French public administration was reorganized by Napoleon and was given a quasi-military structure; it was not the first time that civil public administration had followed military principles, as the military had also been well organized before the existence of states or other administrations. French civil servants wore specially designed costumes; they were hierarchically organized in a structure which allowed redress. In the army, if an individual was not satisfied with decisions taken against his interests, he had the right, even in the absence of any written legal rule, to apply to the person who took the decision, or to his superior and ask for redress. In certain areas, special committees were established to hear cases in a quasi-judicial manner.

The Emperor also created a special council, the Conseil d'Etat, a rationalization and modernization of the pre-existing Conseil du Roi. In tandem with many administrative roles, the Council had the jurisdiction to decide on every case of administrative law brought to its attention with a *recours pour excès de pouvoir*. The decision was not final, but it had the character of a recommendation to the head of the state, the Emperor.

During those times – the times of the Lights – Cartesian rationalization of public powers was the dream of revolutionaries across the world. The so-called Napoleonic state and, in particular, the Napoleonic administration, became famous throughout Europe and beyond. Thanks also to the persuasive force of Napoleon's troops, the system spread around continental Europe.

The administration was organized following the ministerial system, hierarchically and of a monolithic construction. Nothing was outside that system, and everything was meant to be dealt with by the administration, its offices and its officials.

The definition of public administration became one of those most discussed and yet unsolved legal problems. Normally, there was no need for a definition, because public administration was the state par excellence in absolutist times, the pre-existing reality. However, at the time of the triumph of the doctrine of separation of powers, definition could be needed.

Political scientists and lawyers were certainly drawing comfortable conclusions about legislative and judicial powers, their character and their structure. Nevertheless, they experienced difficulties in separating the administration from legislative power; especially since it was recognized that the executive could have rulemaking powers. They had difficulties separating the administration from judicial power because, inevitably, administrative decisions are often a sort of

---

[15] Every book of French administrative law explains that development. Also, S Flogaitis, *Administrative Law et droit administratif* (Paris, LGDJ, 1986); S Cassese, *La construction du droit administratif: France et Royaume-Uni* (Paris, Monchrestien, 2000); also, among others, F Bluche et al, *La Révolution française* (Paris, PUF, Que sais-je, 1989).

adjudication.[16] Still more problematic were difficulties they experienced understanding the nature of the acts of state as a subcategory of the acts of the executive.

This public administration had to wait until after the fall of the Empire of Napoleon III finally to take shape. The dramatic events of the invasion of France by the Prussians (1870–71), the Commune of Paris (18 March and, formally, between 28 March and 28 May 1871), and the establishment of the Third Republic greatly contributed to this shaping process.

One of the first decisions taken by the new regime – following a famous parliamentary debate lead by Léon Gambetta – was to give the Conseil d'Etat the power to decide its cases and no longer to allow it to pronounce recommendations to the head of the state.[17] Under the influence of English liberalism, criticism by the liberals of the nineteenth century against the system of the separation of cases of the administration from cases of the ordinary courts and their subjection to the administration itself was so strong, that the government could do little more than try to save the system. They did this by passing from the system of the *justice retenue*, to the system of the *justice déléguée*[18] and by creating a Tribunal des Conflits.

The year 1873 was destined to remain in the memory of every public lawyer of the continent, as was the name of one little girl, Mademoiselle Blanco.

Mademoiselle Blanco was a little girl who suffered an accident on a street, and was injured by a wagon owned by a manufacturer of tobacco belonging to the

---

[16] Administrative acts which decide a specific case are quasi-judicial in character. On the other hand, very often judicial decisions are of an administrative nature. The distinction between administrative decisions and judicial decisions is a question which has never been – and cannot be – answered. The doctrine produced thousands of pages of legal science dealing with these questions, however, it never produced convincing and generally accepted answers to them, perhaps because none existed. The doctrine was, in fact, trapped within the confines of a dogmatic approach, that of the principle of the separation of powers. Finally, the doctrine concluded that the distinction rather relied on the special guarantees which are given to judges. Nevertheless, this does not answer the questions surrounding the difference in the nature of the two kinds of state actions. It should be noted that this similarity permitted the judiciary of England to extend the prerogative writs to administrative decisions, considered as quasi-judicial decisions.

[17] Among many studies on the Conseil d'Etat, see J-P Costa, *Le Conseil d'Etat dans la société contemporaine* (Paris, Economica, 1993); *Journées d'étude à l'occasion du bicentenaire du code civil, Le Conseil d'Etat et le Code civil* (Paris, Direction des Journaux Officiels, 2004); E Arnoult and F Monnier, *Le Conseil d'Etat. Juger, Conseiller, Servir* (Paris, Gallimard, 1999); R Chapus, *Droit du contentieux administratif*, 13th edn (Paris, Montchrestien, 2008); M Degoffe, *La juridiction administrative spécialisée* (Paris, LGDJ, 1996); O Gohin, *Contentieux administratif*, 6th edn (Paris, Litec, 2010); Y Robinot and D Truchet, *Le Conseil d'Etat* (Paris, PUF, Que sais-je?, 2002); R de Bellescize, *Droit administratif général* (Paris, Gualino, 2013); C-J Hamson, *Executive Discretion and Judicial Control, an Aspect of the French Conseil d'Etat* (London, Stevens, 1954); L Neville-Brown and J Bell, *French Administrative Law* (Oxford, Clarendon Press, 1998).

[18] See, among others, S Cassese, *La construction du droit administratif: France et Royaume-Uni* above n 15 at 35ff and 37ff; C Duval, 'Les justifications de la raison d'être et du maintien de la juridiction administrative en France au XIXe siècle' (1996) 8 *Jahrbuch für europäische Verwaltungsgeschichte* 57; V Wright, 'Le Conseil d'Etat et les changements de régime: le cas du second Empire' (1998) *Revue Administrative* 13; V Wright, 'La réorganisation du Conseil d'Etat en 1872' (1972) 25 *Etudes et Documents du Conseil d'Etat* 21; Neville Brown and J Bell, *French Administrative Law*, 5th edn (Oxford, Oxford University Press, 1998); J Bell, *French Legal Cultures* (Cambridge, Cambridge University Press, 2001); J Bell, *Judiciaries within Europe, a Comparative Review* (Cambridge, Cambridge University Press, 2010).

state yet used by a private company following a contract with the state.[19] Her father took the case to the civil courts asking for damages. The Prefect of Bordeaux objected to the jurisdiction of the civil courts and the case was finally decided by the Tribunal des Conflits, the jurisdiction which was created in order to decide cases of conflict of jurisdiction, both civil and administrative.[20] The Tribunal des Conflits decided that this case was not of the competence of the civil courts, because state liability had to remain exclusively under the rules of public law, public law being the law of public administration.[21]

The science of administrative law was nascent at that time, and time was needed to assess and evaluate the decision bearing the name of the aforementioned little girl, Mlle Blanco. By the dawn of the twentieth century, however, it had become the foundation of administrative law and the science of state.

Up to the decision *Mlle Blanco*, the jurisdiction of the administrative courts resided in case-specific legislative provisions, allowing those courts to declare the state financially responsible for its action, known as the system of the '*Etat-débiteur*'.[22] Following the conclusions of the Commissaire du Gouvernement David – which became even more famous than the decision itself – the ordinary courts found themselves radically without jurisdiction to decide upon any application made against the public administration for the activities of a public service.[23]

It is interesting to note that, at the same time, case law of the Conseil d'Etat was recognizing that apart from administrative decisions – *actes d'autorité* – there were also *actes de gestion*, taken by the so-called *administration domaniale*. This distinction was brought into administrative law by the case law; as the Conseil d'Etat was concerned with litigation produced by allegedly illegal administrative acts, it did not produce a legal theory of that administration's activity, which was of private law. E Laferrière, the founder of French administrative law as a legal science, wrote in the nineteenth century that the *actes de gestion* were motivated by the public interest, nonetheless public power did not intervene.[24] That

---

[19] Following the system called '*regie*', meaning that the state regularly receives a predetermined sum of money.

[20] The Tribunal des Conflits was created at the same time as the system of the *justice retenue* progressed to the system of the *justice déléguée*, because, up until then, conflicts of jurisdiction were decided upon by the Council of State, and the liberals had criticized that system very severely. See, for further detail, all books of French administrative law.

[21] Conclusions of Commissaire du Gouvernement David, D 1873.3, 17; M Long et al, *Les Grands Arrêts de la jurisprudence administrative*, 19th edn (Paris, Dalloz, 2013) 1. The decision on *Blanco* was discovered later, when the conclusions of G Teissier in the case *Feutry* de 1908 were published.

[22] See, eg the decision of the Conseil d'Etat, 6 December 1855, *Rothschild*, Rec 707.

[23] In this way, 'public service' became the criterion of the jurisdiction of the administrative justice.

[24] Laferrière, *Traité de la juridiction administrative et des recours contentieux*, above n 8 at 437, where he writes: 'The contracts concluded by the administration for the functioning of the public services and the realization of works of public interest, the actions taken for the revalorization of the public property, the monetary engagements of the State or by the local authorities in order to face the needs which they have to deal with, they are *actes de gestion*; they are motivated by the public interest, but the public power does intervene'. These are the *Hilfsgeschäfte* of German law. Furthermore, he continues: 'The litigation produced by the acts of the public power is administrative in nature, the litigation produced by the *actes de gestion* is not administrative unless the law so determines'.

distinction was finally well-established as *gestion publique* and *gestion privée*, through the decision of the Tribunal des Conflits, *Compagnie d'assurances le Soleil*, of 1910.[25]

The turn of the century, moreover, witnessed the introduction of many changes to state organization and its law.[26]

During the second half of the eighteenth century, the states realized that much needed economic progress could be greatly enhanced through the development of new innovations of those times, such as electricity, trains, telegraph and telephone communications, amongst others. States developed a specific mode of incorporating such technologies into public purposes, by creating ministries and sub-departments, dedicated to the administration of new technologies which were declared to be of state interest.

It was quickly realized that such ministerial organization and public law were not the best context for activities which were essentially industrial and commercial. Initially, help came in the shape of the extensive use of concessions. By using a contract, a private investor was taking responsibility for developing a certain activity of state interest and expected to be reimbursed with some profit, through the fee payable by those utilizing the activity. This kind of relationship was developed in various ways in order to financially satisfy the private investor. Concessions were – in effect – the first kinds of privatization; this technique came from the *ancien régime*, but it was perfectly fitted to the ideology of the liberal state. Moreover, the state was considered free to choose the investor of its choice, with no restrictions as to the method of selection.[27]

Concessions were organized as a contract of public law; as the state could not alienate its power to regulate, organize and facilitate public services, it was necessary to accept that the state always possessed the power to intervene in the regulatory part of the contract of concession and could alter its content – something that could only be done if the contract was of public law.

Another development at the turn of the twentieth century was the creation of public entities, each detached from the main body of the state, and with responsibility to run a certain state activity under their own name, yet under the umbrella

---

[25] Tribunal des Conflits, 4 June 1910, *Compagnie d'assurances le Soleil*, 466, conclusions Feuillolay, RDP, 1910, 474, conclusions and comments by G Jèze. Also, G Braibant, *Le droit administratif français* (Paris, PFNSP/Dalloz, 1988) 446ff.

[26] A considerable part of this evolution was, in fact, due to the distinction between *actes d'autorité* and *actes de gestion*. The clarity of the distinction owed a great deal to very important deviations introduced by law, in favour of the administrative jurisdiction and – in this way – of public law. The Law of 27 September 1793 introduced the principle according to which the satisfaction of public debts came under administrative jurisdiction. This clause gave rise to the so-called theory of the 'debtor state' (*Etat débiteur*): every time that an administrative action incurred a debt as a consequence, the litigation was brought to the administrative jurisdiction, which, in its turn, had the opportunity to reason under public law. In this way, many cases, which were normally the result of *actes de gestion* were brought to the administrative jurisdiction and to public law. This was especially the case in the domain of the so-called administrative or public contracts. See on this topic, Ch Eisenmann, *Cours de droit administratif*, vol II, (Paris, LGDJ, 1982) 59.

[27] Flogaitis, *Les contrats administratifs*, above n 2 at 87ff, with extended bibliography.

of external state control.[28] Such entities functioned under public law and were called *établissements publics*.

It was understood that there were certain activities which the state wanted to develop in its own name and under its own responsibility, but which could not continue to be included in the ministerial hierarchy. Perhaps unsurprisingly, these were, once again, particular activities which had industrial and commercial aspects, such as the ones mentioned above. They could not be taken out of the realm of public law because, following the decision of the Tribunal des Conflits, *Mlle Blanco*, state activities were necessarily governed by public law. Consequently, the only thing that they could do was to organize them outside the influence of ministerial hierarchy; once again, they thought that they should not break the uniformity of the state administration. This led to a proposed scheme of connections between central administration and those public entities detached from it called tutelage, or *tutelle*. The new system of organization of public administration was called *décentralisation par services* and was always valid.[29]

The tradition of understanding public administration as exclusive to the realm of public law, changed drastically in 1921, just after the end of the First World War, thanks to the decision of the Tribunal des Conflits, *Société commerciale de l'Ouest Africain*, known also as the decision *Bac-d'Eloca*.[30]

In the French colony Côte d'Ivoire, there were several lagoons creating problems for travel and therefore the Colony decided upon, and organized a system of ferry boats, assuring transportation from one side of every lagoon to the other. On the night of 5 to 6 September 1920, an accident occurred and a ferryboat was inverted, causing damage both to people and goods. The case was brought to the attention of the local ordinary judge and (bearing in mind this was post-decision *Blanco*) the Colony objected before the Tribunal des Conflits. This decided that the service assured for transportation across the river was not operating under unilateral state regulation, but under the same conditions as when this kind of service was offered by private individuals. Therefore the responsibility for paying damages should not be included under the umbrella of public law, but rather under private law. Ironically, that decision reflected the opposite of the decision in *Blanco*, which had similarly centred upon an accident concerning transport. The change was due to the fact that half a century had passed since the first decision.

The decision in *Bac-d'Eloca* is very important to the study of public administrations. Rather than negating the character of public service of the ferryboat activity, instead, it reaffirmed it.[31] It also declared that an activity of public administration – a public service – could simultaneously be organized and function

---

[28] S Flogaitis, *La notion de décentralisation en France, en Allemagne et en Italie* (Paris, LGDJ, 1979).

[29] Ibid at 28ff.

[30] Tribunal des Conflits, 22 January 1921, *Société commerciale de l'Ouest Africain*, Rec 91, followed by the decision of the Conseil d'Etat, 23 December 1921, *Société générale d'armement*, Rec 1109; Long et al, *Les Grands arrêts*, above n 21 at 223; Eisenmann, *Cours de droit administratif*, vol I, above n 26.

[31] Conclusions by the Commissaire du Gouvernement Matter.

under private law. From that time forward, public law did not have a monopoly in public administration, because it could also be organized under private law.

This evolution was greatly enhanced after the Second World War, when the use of concessions was developed further. Initially, concessions were meant to be offered only for public services of an industrial or commercial character. Gradually, the case law of the Conseil d'Etat became a clear marker so that additional so-called administrative public services could be conceded. These included, for example, the collection of taxes, hospitals, educational activities and so on.[32]

This development and progress went even further, through the creation of private bodies to run public services, in other words, to aid public interests.

Public Administration and *Fiskus*

The nineteenth century was, for France, a period of her history which was characterized by political changes of all sorts. However, the political legacy of the Revolution was omnipresent, even in the times of Empire. In the neighbouring Germany, history and the modernization of the state took another path; at the root of this divergence was the absolutism, which lasted longer.

In an absolutist state, it was unthinkable to challenge the authority of an administrative act. Public administration was the powerful extended hand of the sovereign, the full weight of its authority was felt. Challenging the authority of an administrative act would be equal to challenging the unassailable authority of the Prince.

This underscored the reason why, when the Conseil d'Etat was developing a true administrative law system in the final quarter of the nineteenth century, the German courts did not follow suit. It was the doctrine which eventually ushered in change and important authors, led by Professor Otto Mayer,[33] developed a scientific dialogue on administrative law. Ever since, the German doctrine of administrative law has enjoyed precedence over the case law of the courts.[34]

Those were the days of the so-called *Pandektenrecht*, when an excellent school of thought arose through the work of Savigny[35] and Mommsen,[36] prestigious

---

[32] Flogaitis, *Les contrats administratifs*, above n 2 at 87ff.

[33] Otto Mayer was the founder of German administrative law. He was Professor at the University of Strasbourg, during a time when that region belonged to Germany. He wrote his book, *Le droit administratif allemand*, in the French language, paying tribute to the legal system of his inspiration. Ever since, he has been considered to be a symbol of the dialogue between the two public law systems.

[34] The most recent example are the three volumes edited by W Hoffmann-Riem, E Schmidt-Aßmann and A Voßkuhle, *Grundlagen des Verwaltungsrechts*, vol I: *Methoden, Maßstäbe, Aufgaben, Organisation*, 2nd edn (2012); vol II: *Informationsordnung, Verwaltungsverfahren, Handlungsformen* 2nd edn (2012); vol III: *Personal, Finanzen, Kontrolle, Sanktionen, Staatliche Einstandspflichten*, 2nd edn (2013).

[35] FK von Savigny, *System des heutigen römischen Rechts* (Berlin, Veit, 1840), reprinted by Scientia Verlag, Aalen, 1973.

[36] T Mommsen, *Abriss des römischen Staatsrechts* (Leipzig, Duncker und Humblot, 1907).

professors who revived the spirit of Roman law within what is known as the historic school of law.

As it was impossible to challenge the authority of an administrative act, the civil law courts, under the influence of the doctrine, started developing case law concerned with the financial consequences of illegal administrative acts. To that end they brought back the concept of *Fiscus* of Roman law, which was significantly re-shaped and transformed into *Fiskus*.

At the beginning, they taught that *Fiskus* was a separate legal individual from the Prince or the state,[37] and one which had to address damage created by the illegal acts of the Prince. In this way, the revival of the concept of *Fiscus* made its own contribution to the development of the state ruled by law, even if it was to the civil law.[38] At the same time, it contributed to the conviction of the legal theory and practice which asserts that there are areas of state action where civil law is the natural law.[39]

In Otto Mayer's lifetime, and largely thanks to his work, this was more sharply clarified. The state was no longer considered to be composed of two facets, one of public law and another of private law (*Fiskus*). Instead, it was considered as a double-faceted institution, acting – following the famous phrase of Walter Jellinek – at times, as a private person (*in Zivil*) and sometimes as a public authority, in uniform (*in Uniform*).[40] The concept of *Fiskus* was accepted by the Reichsgericht in 1884;[41] subsequently, every activity of the state which created differences of a financial nature became the competence of the civil jurisdiction. On 12 March 1918, the Reichsgericht rationalized its position[42] and abandoned the theory of *Fiskus*, by introducing the concept of civil litigation (*bürgerliche Rechtsstreitigkeit*) in the place of the litigation of civil law (*zivilrechtliche Streitigkeit*). This also embraced litigation originating in public law.

---

[37] A distinction was introduced between the state as a figure of public law, producing acts of authority, and the state as *Fiskus*, a figure of private law, as explained by Mayer, *Le droit administratif allemand*, vol I, above n 3 at 57–58. It can be compared with some aspects of the English legal traditions; see mainly EH Kantorowicz, *The King's Two Bodies, a Study in Medieval Political Theology* (Princeton, Princeton University Press, 1957) 164ff; FW Maitland, 'The Crown's Corporate Sole' in *Selected Essays* (Cambridge, Cambridge University Press, 1936) 104ff.

[38] This was first underlined by G Jellinek, *System der subjektiven öffentlichen Rechte* (Tübingen, Mohr (P Siebeck), 1905) 60ff.

[39] P Laband, *Das Staatsrecht des deutschen Reiches* (Tübingen, Mohr (P Siebeck), 1911–14).

[40] W Jellinek, *Verwaltungsrecht* (Berlin/Zürich, Gehlen, 1966) (reproduction from the 3rd edn of 1931) at 25.

[41] RGZ 11, 65, RGZ 22, 285, E Forsthoff, *Lehrbuch des Verwaltungsrechts*, vol I (Allgemeiner Teil, München, Beck, 1973) 115.

[42] RGZ 92, 310; E Forsthoff, ibid.

The Development of a Public Administration in England

England of the eighteenth century was characterized by an almost total absence of central administration.[43] The central state was gradually created around the institution of the Crown, which, because it was personified, made it difficult – if not impossible – to create a general theory of state, because, of course, the state was itself a personified institution. Such a task proved even more difficult because of the special position of the Crown among public institutions, the flexibility of its position within the political history of the country, as well as the determination of Parliament – which had inherited the powers of the Crown – to keep absolute power for itself. In fact, sovereignty in the sense of the imposition of the will of the state internally in the country, the power (the *Herrschaft* as taught by the German lawyers in the nineteenth century) originally the remit of the King as a physical person, passed to Parliament. This meant that it did not pass to the people but to the institution representing them, and Parliament never agreed to power-sharing. If the judges acquired an unrivalled importance within this institutional framework, it was because they also inherited a distinctive, autonomous portion of the internal sovereign power of the King. England was a unique case in Europe, where centralization of the powers around the Crown was not meant to be facilitated through a powerful centralized administration, but rather through the judiciary. The perception of the King's presence and power in England owed a great debt to the judges who administered justice throughout the kingdom in the name of the King.[44]

The administrative powers were executed around the country by the justices of peace, who had a mixture of powers, administrative and judicial. If, however, the justices of peace performed these various duties until the nineteenth century, change was afoot. The embryonic English public administration, the development of what they called 'collectivism', was beginning to impose new forms of organizing and executing public powers. The Factory Act 1802, the Reform Act 1867, and especially the Local Government Act 1871 – which created, inter alia, the Local Government Board, and was consolidated by the Public Health Acts of 1872 and 1875 – constituted the foundations of the modern administrative machinery of England.[45]

At the same time, the institutions of local government started expanding. Local government – as conceived at the beginning and consolidated in later centuries – consisted of the nationwide organization of boroughs and counties. These were entities with dual identity; they had legal personality of their own and were, simultaneously, organs of the Crown.[46]

---

[43] Giannini, *Il pubblico potere*, above n 1 at 30.
[44] Flogaitis, *Administrative Law et droit administratif*, above n 15 at 59ff.
[45] Ibid at 63ff where there is also further useful bibliography.
[46] Flogaitis, *La notion de décentralisation en France, en Allemagne et en Italie*, above n 28, where this issue is analyzed, especially in the light of German law and the monumental work of von Gneist.

Public Administration of States and other 'Public' or 'Private' Administrations

Argument pertaining to the development of public administration thus far highlights the idea that public administration, as developed in continental countries, did not always come under the realm of public law. Modern public administrations may be governed by rules of public or private law in a far less differentiated way. The term 'public' does not imply public law, as may be erroneously presumed, but refers, instead, to the general interest of the public and organized society, to which public administration should always offer its services.[47] The modern German doctrine has codified the principle and rules of public administration acting in private law under the term 'private administrative law' (*Privatverwaltungsrecht*).[48]

It should not be forgotten, however, that this private law is not identical to the one governing the relations of private individuals, especially because public administration, whether acting under public or private law, is always bound by the obligation to serve the public interest and – in particular – to observe the constitution. These necessities overlay the hues of public law upon private administrative law.[49]

States, however, do not have a monopoly on administrations. Administrations have developed in various different ways, and some of them merit the adjective 'public'. Examples of other kinds of administrations include the following eight:

a) First, there are international administrations,[50] which reflect the character of international organizations; their numbers continue to grow.

These international organizations are created by international treaty, according to the special provisions. They may, for instance, be political, scientific or cultural. The most important of all of them, because of its global aim, is the United Nations (UN) organization. Very important international organizations with complex administrative structures also include those of

---

[47] This is a very pertinent observation which has already been made by MS Giannini in his *Diritto amministrativo* (Milano, Giuffrè, 1970).

[48] See all books of German administrative law and, in particular, D Ehlers, *Verwaltung in Privatrechtsform* (Berlin, Duncker und Humblot, 1984); C Franchini and BG Mattarella (a cura di), *Sabino Cassese e i confini del diritto amministrativo* (Napoli, Editoriale Scientifica, 2011).

[49] Flogaitis, *Les contrats administratifs*, above n 2 at 213ff; L Ortega, 'L'evoluzione delle basi costituzionali del diritto amministrativo' in M d'Alberti (a cura di), *Le nuove mete del diritto amministrativo* (Bologna, Il Mulino, 2010) 143.

[50] A von Bogdandy et al (eds), *The Exercise of Public Authority by International Institutions, Advancing International Institutional Law* (Heidelberg, New York, Springer, 2010); E Schmidt-Aßmann, 'Die Herausforderung der Verwaltungsrechtswissenschaft durch die Internationalisierung der Verwaltungsbeziehungen' (2006) 45 *Der Staat* 315; R Collins and ND White (eds), *International Organizations and the Idea of Autonomy, Institutional Independence in the International Legal Order* (Abingdon, New York, Routledge, 2011).

military character, with NATO (North Atlantic Treaty Organization) as perhaps the most important of them.[51]

International organizations, and especially the UN, have well-developed
public administration around the globe. The rules pertaining to that public
administration are agreed by the political organs of the organization. In the
main, they reflect the standards of the most advanced public administrations
of the Member States. In fact, international civil service aims to attract the
highest performing professionals from around the world and be the leading
example for all other modern public administration. A comprehensive grievance system protects both civil servants of the UN and those of any other
international organization against any arbitrariness of public management.[52]

b) Administrations of various types which operate above and beyond the state,[53]
    for example, international professional associations of all kinds,[54] cultural
    organizations and – perhaps most significant of all – sports associations. The
    latter organize sports activities all over the world. In doing so, they have direct
    power which is sometimes also of a judicial nature: they can take action and
    adopt repressive measures against sports societies without the need for refer-
    ence either to states or state administrations.[55]

c) There is administration of regional organizations and, in particular, of the
    European Union.

---

[51] There is an extended bibliography about international organizations and, more specifically, on
international civil service, its role, development and legal status. See, among others: H Mouritzen, *The
International Civil Service, a Study of Bureaucracy: International Organizations* (Dartmouth, Aldershot,
1990); Y Beigbeder, *Threats to the International Civil Service* (London, Pinter, 1988); A Plantey, *The
International Civil Service, Law and Management* (New York, Masson, 1981); AC Damsgaard, *Staffing
an International Civil Service, Principles and Practice, the United Nations Secretariat* (Copenhagen,
Political Studies Press, 1983); NA Graham and RS Jordan, *The International Civil Service, Changing
Roles and Concepts* (New York, Pergamon, 1980); CF Amerasinghe, *The Law of the International Civil
Service, as Applied by International Administrative Tribunals* (Oxford, Clarendon Press, 1994).

[52] United Nations Administrative Tribunal, *International Administrative Tribunals in a Changing
World* (London, Esperia, 2008); S Flogaitis, 'I principi generali del diritto nella giurisprudenza del
Tribunale Amministrativo delle Nazioni Unite' in M d'Alberti, *Le nuove mete del diritto amministrativo,*
above n 49 at 93ff.

[53] See, among others, A Obser, *Communicative Structuration and Governance of the Global
Environment through Policy Networks of International Aid Organizations* (Baden-Baden, Nomos, 1999);
HG Gemuenden, T Ritter and A Walter, *Relationships and Networks in International Markets* (Oxford,
Pergamon, 1997); ME Keck and K Sikkink, *Activists beyond Borders, Advocacy Networks in International
Politics* (London, Cornell University Press, 1998); H Bakis, R Abler and EM Roche, *Corporate Networks,
International Telecommunications, and Interdependence, Perspectives from Geography and Information
Systems* (London, Belhaven Press, 1993); BH Erickson, *International Networks, the Structured Webs of
Diplomacy and Trade* (Beverly Hills, Sage, 1975).

[54] See, eg R Fisher, *Arts Networking in Europe, the Second Directory of Trans-national Cultural
Networks, Associations, and International Non-governmental Organizations in Europe* (London, ACGB,
1997).

[55] See, among others, R Giulianotti and R Robertson, *Globalization and Sport* (Oxford, Blackwell,
2007); P Millword, *The Global Football League, Transnational Networks, Social Movements and Sport in
the New Media Age* (Basingstoke, Palgrave Macmillan, 2011); J Soek, *The Strict Liability Principle and
the Human Rights of Athletes in Doping Cases* (The Hague, Asser, 2006).

The European Union has two administrations, one direct and one indi-rect.[56] The direct administration of the European Union consists of all civil servants employed directly by it and working for the advancement of the European policies. Apart from the international civil service, the European Union also uses the public administrations of its Member States to aid the advancement of its purposes. In this way, they become indirect administra-tions of the European Union.[57]

d) There are professional associations. The most important of these are the trade unions, because they represent – in a precise and organized way – large swathes of the population as well as specific economic interests and activities. Apart from the trade unions, however, there are many other professional organizations of all kinds reflecting this key feature of representing collective interests.

e) In all modern democratic states, political parties have become true public powers and have developed administrations of their own, while simultane-ously being part of international networks and party associations. This is an entirely new development. Today, political parties are entities with political, constitutional and administrative functions, demonstrating the exercise of public power at various intra-state levels, but also internationally.[58]

f) Public administrations of all kinds and levels have also created international networks which quite often have normative powers of their own, reaching beyond the direct control of states. When those networks are constituted by independent administrative authorities, they are completely beyond any state control.[59]

g) There are Church administrations, and administrations of religious organiza-tions.

The Christian Churches developed an administration of their own dating back to the first days of their existence. For centuries, the Catholic Church

---

[56] J Schwarze, *Europäisches Verwaltungsrecht*, 2nd edn (Baden-Baden, Nomos, 2005).

[57] P Craig, 'Amministrazione Comunitaria. Storia, tipologia e "accountability"' in d'Alberti, above n 49 at 11; S Cassese, *Lo spazio giuridico globale* (Roma-Bari, Laterza, 2003) 27ff.

[58] The European political parties, which are associations of political parties acting nationally, have their own administrative structure, and although they do not constitute rigid structures, they serve a vital purpose because they serve as a platform for the personal networking of politicians in an interna-tional environment. The same applies to the international parties. See, S Henig and J Pinder (eds), *European Political Parties* (London, Allen and Unwin, 1969); R Morgan and St Silvestri (eds), *Moderates and Conservatives in Western Europe, Political Parties, the European Community and the Atlantic Alliance* (London, Heinemann Educational, 1982); G Pridham and P Pridham, *Towards Transnational Parties in the European Community* (London, Policy Studies Institute, 1979); G Pridham and P Pridham, *Transnational Party Cooperation and European Integration, the Process towards Direct Elections* (London, Allen and Unwin, 1981); J Gaffney, *Political Parties and the European Union* (London, Routledge, 1996); M Leonard, *Politics without Frontiers, the Role of Political Parties in Europe's Future* (London, Demos, 1997); DS Bell and C Lord (eds), *Transnational Parties in the European Union* (Aldershot, Ashgate, 1998); R Ladrech, *Europeanization and Political Parties, towards a Framework for Analysis* (Keele University, 2001); RM Goldman (ed), *Transnational Parties, Organizing the World's Precincts* (Lanham, MD and London, University Press of America, 1983).

[59] S Rose-Ackerman and PL Lindseth (eds), *Comparative Administrative Law* (Cheltenham, Edward Elgar, 2010).

was the only institution in Western Europe with an administration both serving its interests and promoting its objectives. Today, all major Churches and
other religions have well-structured administrations.[60]

h)   There are large commercial companies with – arguably – the most important
administrations of modern times. These include huge commercial companies, especially those of international dimension, for instance Coca-Cola, or
British Petroleum. Several of these are state-owned companies, or companies
with state interests of one kind or another invested in them.

   These are well-structured administrations, demonstrating best practice,
and developed in all kinds of environments. They are often more powerful
than the states which host them, not only in terms of the means at their dis-
posal, but chiefly because – amongst other attributes – of their organizational
capacity, professionalism, modern structures and efficiency.[61]

The administrations described here, plus others, constitute – in conjunction
with state administration – a form of modern ensemble state administration,
which – from the point of view of an administrative lawyer or of an administrative
scientist – seem to by-pass conventional definitions of public or private.

They are governed by commonly-agreed best practice and by principles and
values which also are common to all of them in a globalized world. These administrations have given rise to global administrative law,[62] a new approach to administrative law, through which all sorts of administrations are studied horizontally
and from a common point of view.

The Divide between Public Law and Private Law

Public law, as it emerged throughout modern state history, had felt the impact of
the French Revolution and Napoleon, who consolidated its doctrine into specific
institutions. They chose to maintain public law as the law of the state and, most
specifically, of public administration. This choice would probably not have had

---

[60] eg E Chiti, *The Administrative Law of the Roman Catholic Church, A Comparative Inquiry* (New York University, Jean Monnet Working Paper 12/2010).

[61] There are many studies in that area, eg J Coates, EW Davis and RJ Stacey, *Managerial Short-termism in Multi-national Companies, the Role of a Distributed Corporate Performance Measurement System* (Birmingham, Ashton Business School Research Institute, 1994).

[62] Global administrative law is a novelty, as a concept and term. It was proposed by two scholars of the New York University, Professor Richard Stewart and Benedict Kingsbury, and rapidly expanded all over the world. Professor Sabino Cassese of the University of Rome 'La Sapienza' with his works as well as the works of his followers, along with others, lent further legal content to the concept and global administrative law started being developed in law faculties worldwide. See, among others, G Antony (ed), *Values in Global Administrative Law* (Oxford, Hart Publishing, 2011); AJ Aman, *Administrative Law in a Global Era* (London, Cornell University Press, 1992); S Monnt, *State Liability in Investment Treaty Arbitration, Global Constitutional and Administrative Law in the BIT Generation* (Oxford, Hart Publishing, 2009); V Goshal, *Reforming Rules and Regulations. Laws, Institutions and Implementations* (Cambridge, MA and London, MIT Press, 2010).

the effect that we know if the revolutionaries and Napoleon had not adamantly refused to permit the judiciary to judge the administrative action.

We need to examine this decision in order more fully to understand its impact. It was decided that whoever had a grievance against public administration would bring it by *recours pour excès de pouvoir* to the attention of the Conseil d'Etat. Moreover, it was decided that a number of cases of litigation with the public administration would be decided upon by the Conseils de Préfecture or other specified public bodies. Equally all cases of civil liberties, in what was called *voie de fait*, were entrusted to ordinary justice being considered the natural protector of them. That meant that what the reformers had in mind in terms of litigation, and what they attributed to both ordinary courts or administrative adjudication, did not conform to the doctrinal division between public law and private law. Instead, it was determined by the concern that certain litigation did not come under the jurisdiction of the ordinary courts. The submission by the law of cases, especially under the competence of the Conseils de Préfecture, was empirical and there is plenty of evidence to be found of this in the case of the contracts of public works.[63]

It was only later – mainly after 1872 – that the case law of the Conseil d'Etat and of the Tribunal des Conflits, supported by legal theory, started trying to provide a doctrinal explanation for the reasons why a series of kinds of litigation were attributed to the administrative jurisdiction and not to the ordinary courts. In many cases attempts to provide explanations failed.[64] Nonetheless, it was the law that distributed the litigation between the jurisdictions in France and the Tribunal des Conflits which bore responsibility for those choices.

In several other countries of the continent and around the world which had followed French solutions, things may have developed differently, because the constitutions adopted more rigid variations of the same system. This happened, for example, in Germany after the Second World War, where the organization of the courts into branches was made by the Constitution itself, thus necessitating interpretations of constitutional value because of the division between public law and private law. The same happened in Greece, which followed the German options on this point.

English administrative law, however, remained unaffected by the pace and patterns in the historical developments of administrative law on the continent. It had enjoyed the comparative luxury of starting seriously to develop apace in times when all the doctrinal battles about the public law and private law divide had lost their political significance and the issue had acquired a rather technical character in the countries of its origin. After all, big portions of public administration in those countries of its origin were now given over, or left to, private law. Moreover, England and English law had developed over the centuries without any need to exploit the distinction between public law and private law, because of the unitary jurisdiction of the ordinary courts.

---

[63] See in detail: S Flogaitis, *Les contrats administratifs*, above n 2.
[64] Ibid.

It is important to stress at this point, nevertheless, that the common belief that English law does not distinguish between rules of public law and those of private law is untrue. The distinction exists by itself in any case, because the state has rules of organization, tax laws, or those for defence and security, and so on. In other words, it has the power to act unilaterally and to impose its will on private individuals without asking permission to do so, and that is the essential core of public law. Nonetheless, it has not needed to recognize the distinction for jurisdictional purposes or, to be precise, it did not need to recognize it until very recently.

This change came about because of the decision of the House of Lords in *O'Reilly v Mackman*,[65] which introduced the *novum* in English law that, when a case questions the legality of an administrative decision of a public body, that case should be brought to court through the – new for its time – procedure, *the judicial review of administrative action*. Suddenly, the legal system which had, for centuries, considered itself free of such vestiges of history, needed to invent the public law and private law divide and find ways to define public bodies, in other words, authorities producing administrative decisions.[66] Order 53 of the Rules of Court declared itself applicable in cases of decisions taken 'in the exercise of a public function'.

It was ironic in the light of history, because English administrative law had developed a great deal in the 1960s and 1970s thanks to the use of declaration, which was a procedure of 'common' law allowing discovery. Now, the declaration was included among the possibilities of the new application, not allowing use of discovery under the same terms as in 'common law'.

Order 53 introduced a new procedure, the application for judicial review, modernizing and adapting to modern needs, writs, remedies and procedures which had existed without this challenge for centuries. It is not clear from the Order itself whether it was meant to be an exclusive means of law or not. It could be argued that, as the declaration was included among the six remedies to be sought through an application for judicial review, it was no longer possible to use declaration outside it. Nonetheless, this theory is supported by the detail of Order 53.

We need to look more closely at this detail in order to evaluate its impact. Order 53 encompassed six remedies in one principal procedure, the application for judicial review. The first four remedies constitute the core of the new procedure, composed of the ex-prerogative orders, *certiorari*, prohibition, *mandamus* and the ex-injunction of Section 9 of the Administration of Justice (Miscellaneous Provisions) Act 1938. According to the letter of Order 53, these remedies could not be offered except through an application for judicial review ('An application for judicial review *must* be made if the applicant is seeking. . .'). That solution was

---

[65] *O'Reilly v Mackman* (1983) 2 AC 237.

[66] See, among others, HWR Wade and CF Forsyth, *Administrative Law*, 10th edn (Oxford, Oxford University Press, 2009) 566, where the question is dealt with as the divorce of public and private law; D Foulkes, *Administrative Law*, 8th edn (London, Butterworths, 1995) 362; P Craig, *Administrative Law*, 6th edn (London, Sweet and Maxwell, 2008); see also the excellent argument of C Harlow and R Rawlings, in *Law and Administration (Law in Context)*, 3rd edn (New York, Cambridge University Press, 2009).

self-evident because of the history of the four remedies. The other two, however, (the declaration as well as the injunction which does not come under Section 9 mentioned above) could be offered through an application for judicial review ('An application for judicial review *may* be made if the applicant is seeking. . .'). This solution adopted by Order 53 was well-balanced, particularly because a procedure for a declaration under Order 53 would not have the same procedural flexibility accorded to the declaration under common law, especially in the contentious area of the use of discovery.

The House of Lords, by deciding against the letter and the spirit of the first article of Order 53, suddenly brought the necessity, to English law, of defining 'public action', in other words, to the position which French law found itself in during 1872, when the Tribunal des Conflits decided the case *Mlle Blanco*. English Law lost the comparative advantage which history had guaranteed it but, beyond that, citizens seeking declaration in cases of acts of 'public functions' experience less protection than the one guaranteed to them by the law.[67]

---

[67] Flogaitis, *Administrative Law et droit administratif,* above n 15.

Lesson 3

The 'Modern' State and its Foundations: The Rule of Law

During the nineteenth century, the public lawyers developed their ideas for what they used to call the modern state, and for which – as is evidenced from their writings – they were full of admiration[1].

In the case of France, as well as that of the United States of America, the introduction of the modern state was the result of a particular philosophy, the so-called philosophy of the Lights, as well as of a revolution which represented those ideas. In the particular case of the USA, the revolution took the form of a War of Independence. In the case of France, it was the Revolution, promoted by certain forces of society, which mobilized the nation against the so-called *ancien régime*.[2] The French state was modelled by Napoleon, who consolidated the ideas of the Revolution and translated them into state institutions. Moreover, he contributed a great deal to the expansion of what were referred to throughout Europe at that time as Napoleonic institutions and state.

The other important example of a state built during the nineteenth century was the German Empire. In this case, the reform and modernization of structures were not the result of a revolution, but the result of the action of the state itself, from above.[3]

Nineteenth-century Europe was, in effect, a laboratory of new, 'rational', 'modern' institutions and structures. Strangely for continental Europe, the political theories and practices which changed the concept and function of state did not come from the continent but from England, a country which – as we have seen in previous discussion – did not develop a comprehensive theory of state.

[1] eg L Duguit, *Law in the Modern State* (tr F Laski and HJ Laski, BW Huebsch, 1919); G Jellinek, *Allgemeine Staatslehre*, (Kronberg, Athenaeum, 1976) (reprinted from the 3rd edn of 1931); W Jellinek, *Verwaltungsrecht* (Berlin/Zürich, Gehlen, 1966) (reproduction from the 3rd edn of 1913); P Laband, *Das Staatsrecht des deutschen Reiches*, 4th edn (Tübingen, Mohr (P Siebeck), 1911–13).

[2] Many books and contributions of all sorts have been written about the French Revolution of 1789; see, among them, F Bluche, S Rials and J Tulard, *La Révolution Française* (Paris, PUF, Que sais-je? 1989).

[3] S Flogaitis, *La notion de décentralisation en France, en Allemagne et en Italie* (Paris, LGDJ, 1979), and further bibliography cited there.

The French Revolution of 1789 and the Rule of Law[4]

The French Revolution of 1789 served to reform a state which was absolutist. The revolutionaries chose to combine elements originating from the state of the *ancien régime* with others originating from the political philosophy and practice of England.

They chose to preserve the machinery of the state and, more in particular, public administration from the *ancien régime*, which was especially powerful because it was armed with public law. The Revolution needed that machinery first in order to crush all oppositional reaction, throughout the country, to its goals. At the same time, the French Revolution needed to produce a powerful administration, especially because it was so important to unify an extended territory.[5]

The Revolution reaffirmed public law as the law of state administration and, in the name of the principle of the separation of powers, exonerated the public administration from any judicial control. The revolutionaries knew that the judiciary of the *ancien régime* had stopped several of the King's attempts to reform the country, and they were afraid that this could happen again. The administration was powerful and needed to remain powerful in order to be effective. They took some very important steps, which the liberals criticized. In particular, they exonerated civil servants from any responsibility for their actions, and they created a system in which the administration would be the only judge of litigation arising from its activities.

The most important institution to facilitate this was the Conseil d'Etat, established by Napoleon,[6] to advise the Emperor on every administrative issue the law had under its jurisdiction, and especially in rulemaking at all levels and of all sorts. Moreover, it would have jurisdiction to decide on the legality of administrative acts and to recommend to the Emperor the annulment of illegal administrative acts.[7] The Conseil d'Etat was, in an original way, a peculiar institution demonstrating a mix of administrative and judicial powers.[8]

The innovation was the rule of law which the French Revolution brought from England to the continent. Most striking was the sense of the supremacy of the law

---

[4] A Laquièze, 'Etat de droit e sovranità nazionale in Francia' in P Costa and D Zolo (eds), *Lo Stato di diritto: storia, teoria, critica* (Milano, Feltrinelli, 2006) 260.

[5] Flogaitis, *La notion de décentralisation*, above n 3; S Cassese, *La construction du droit administratif. France et Royaume-Uni* (Paris, Monchrestien, 2000).

[6] J Bourdon (ed), *Napoléon au Conseil d'Etat: Notes et procès-verbaux inédits de Jean Guillaume Locre, secrétaire général du Conseil d'Etat* (Paris, Berger-Levrault, 1963).

[7] J Bell, *Judiciaries within Europe, a Comparative Review* (Cambridge, Cambridge University Press, 2010).

[8] The Conseil d'Etat is perhaps the most exported French institution worldwide. It remains true, however, that it was the least exportable French institution; none of its copies was able to reproduce the very characteristic French attitude towards the state and the administration.

vis-à-vis all the powers within the state, including the state itself.[9] Although AV Dicey argues that French public law has nothing to do with the English concept of the rule of law, it is nonetheless true that – thanks to the French Revolution – this very concept changed the public law of the continent, and indeed of the world, forever.

The absolutist state was an innovation and a progression in the history of Europe. It could be regarded as progress because European societies were organized according to new, modern, and often codified rules, which covered almost all aspects of public and private life. After centuries without the existence of a *regime* of state, a new era had begun.[10] The state was governed by public law and was therefore powerful. The motivation of every state activity was the fulfillment of the public interest and therefore all aspects of public interest would be the concern of the state. The rules existed, but when the state applied them, it had the choice to deviate from them in the name of public interest. That was why the term *Polizeistaat* became synonymous with an arbitrary and capricious government.

England was the only European country which had not experienced these developments. Instead, it was governed by the rule of law, as developed over centuries. Moreover, throughout the eighteenth and nineteenth centuries, England had been the metropolis of many ideas, initiatives, developments in political thought and institutional developments. It was hardly surprising, therefore, that the French revolutionaries admired English philosophy and the rule of law; it was equally inevitable that they would choose to adapt such concepts to their own doctrines and philosophy. The French Revolution was proclaimed in the name of the people or, in their words, the nation. They took the concept of the nation from ancient Greece and re-worked it to suit their culture. In Greek, the concept of nation meant ethnicity whereas, in the terminology of the French Revolution, it meant the people, all the citizens of a given state.

They put the nation in the place of the ex-sovereign King; consequently, sovereignty belonged to the nation personified. The nation expressed itself through the elected Parliament and the laws it decided upon. The nation elected the Parliament, which represented the nation, and Parliament decided upon the laws governing the state. As the laws were – albeit through representation – the will of the sovereign, everyone had to obey the law, including the state itself as it had primary responsibility for public administration.

Public administration was known to have been almost synonymous with the state in the absolutist years, effectively the extended hand of the Crown. It had to acknowledge and reflect change, that – in the new *regime* – power belonged to the people and that the executive was a 'permitted' power, which acquired demo-

---

[9] It is generally accepted that the state of law was introduced by the French Revolution, eg R Carré de Malberg, *Contribution à la théorie générale de l'Etat*, 1st edn (Paris, Sirey, 1920) 489; G Burdeau, *Traité de science politique*, vol IV (Paris, LGDJ, 1964) 88. This is only true, however, for the development of law in continental Europe and the countries influenced by the French Revolution.

[10] Among others, MS Giannini, *Il pubblico potere, Stati e amministrazioni pubbliche* (Bologna, Il Mulino, 1986).

cratic legitimacy only through subjection to the laws. It was, in other words, the will of the people expressed through Parliament.[11] This was the core concept of the principle of legality (*principe de légalité*), meaning that, in those times, the public administration could only act on the permission of an Act of Parliament.

The meaning of the principle of legality has evolved in many different ways since that time. The administration no longer acts only if invited to by an Act of Parliament; moreover, it has a democratic legitimacy of its own.[12] That being said, the content of the principle of legality differs from country to country according to its historical legacy and its constitutional background.

The Ideas of AV Dicey, the Rule of Law and the Principle of Legality[13]

AV Dicey[14] belongs to that generation of lawyers which characterized the nineteenth century as the golden age for legal science and important monographs. His book, *Introduction to the Study of the Law of the Constitution,* is characterized by all the advantages and disadvantages – encompassing the strengths and weaknesses – of the important books of law of that century. It could be seen as a comprehensive exploration of the notion and the structures of modern ideas of the state.[15] In those years, distinguished professors and judges from all over Europe wanted to propose doctrines which would be complete and national, especially to

---

[11] This is at the basis of the idea governing administrative law, which possibly continued up to the end of the Second World War, according to which, administrative law was an exceptional body of rules – a '*droit d'exception*' – rules that the state has conceded by exception to its prerogative not to be subject to anyone. For a long period, it was considered that administrative law was a body of rules which developed as exceptions which were graciously offered by the incumbent power to the citizens. See, among others, O Kahn-Freund, C Levy and B Rudden, *A Source-book on French Law: Systems, Methods, Outline of Contracts* (Oxford, Clarendon Press, 1991); GA Bermann and E Picard (eds), *Introduction to French Law* (Alphen aan den Rijn, Kluwer, 2008).

[12] S Flogaitis, *Les contrats administratifs* (London, Esperia, 1998) and further bibliography cited there.

[13] E Santoro, 'Rule of Law e "libertà degli inglesi", L'interpretazione di Albert Venn Dicey' in Costa and Zolo (eds*), Lo Stato di diritto,* above n 4 at 173.

[14] AV Dicey, *Introduction to the Study of the Law of the Constitution,* 8th edn (London, Macmillan, 1915), reprinted (Indianapolis, Liberty Fund Inc, 1982).

[15] Quite often, Dicey is studied as a scientist who proposed a number of personal ideas, especially in reference to the rule of law and the *droit administratif.* This is not exact. All liberal public lawyers of the second half of the nineteenth century throughout Europe shared the same ideas. What needs to be examined is whether they all followed Dicey or whether all of them – Dicey included – concurred with the same school of thought. The best examples are the French lawyers of that time, especially those of the Third Empire, and the Greek liberals, who also wrote critiques of the French system of duality of jurisdictions and who participated in the revolution of 1862 against King Otto of Greece, which led to the Constitution of 1864 and the abolition of the Conseil d'Etat. It should also be borne in mind that the democratic development of the *droit administratif* started after 1872, with the abolition of the system of *justice retenue* and the introduction of the Tribunal des Conflits. Since then, the *droit administratif* began its glorious evolution from protector of public administration to protector of the citizens.

help define their otherness from antagonistic nations. When it came to England, that desire could easily have been pride.[16]

Inspired by liberal ideas, Whig by conviction, and politically engaged, Dicey was very proud of his cultural heritage, although he could never accept his country's evolution towards the welfare state after 1900. By reading between the lines of his book in its various editions, we can see the changes being ushered in by the passing of time. There is a clear change of style, even suggesting a certain incoherence between the first and the last editions.[17] He gradually moves from the polemic tones of his first edition, to a shift of position in the last edition, where he shares his understanding of the erroneous positions of his early days. Interestingly, however, he never repudiates his youth. English pride and certain superior feelings towards the France of the post-Napoleonic era are at the root of his erroneous considerations. His style reveals the British loathing of Napoleon and his legacy to his country and the world.

Dicey's rejection of French administrative law was made through his analysis of the rule of law, the latter having a central role in his work. His analysis was of a comparative character, as was always the case with important treatises of those times. He chose the French *droit administratif* for his comparison, proposing that the rule of law was an English proposal, whilst France was proposing the *droit administratif*. In his view, this was a legal system from which England had been spared thanks to the virtues of the nation which had also saved the country from the Star Chamber and the Stuarts.[18]

There is a qualitative change in what Dicey writes against French *droit administratif* between the fifth and sixth editions of his book, because of his article in the *Law Quarterly Review* of 1901, entitled 'Droit Administratif in Modern French Law'[19]. The substance of that article appeared in two notes in the Appendix of the sixth edition of his book under the titles 'English Misconceptions as to *Droit Administratif*' and 'The evolution of *Droit Administratif*' and was later incorporated into the book itself. During those years, André Batut and Gaston Jèze undertook the French translation of the fifth edition of Dicey's book. Bizarrely, in the Preface to the French edition, Dicey seems to be another man: initial pride cedes

---

[16] S Flogaitis, *Administrative Law et droit administratif* (Paris, LGDJ, 1986) ch I, 'Dicey et le droit administratif' 33.

[17] Although Dicey cites German authors – especially R von Gneist – he is more familiar with the French and American bibliographies. Among the French authors he is particularly familiar with Léon Duguit and Gaston Jèze, with whom he established relationships. He also collaborated with André Colaneri, who gave him important information about the then recent French legislation demonstrating the development of socialist ideas. This information was offered by the author in his book, AV Dicey, *Lectures on the Relation between Law and Public Opinion in England during the Nineteenth Century* (London, Macmillan, 1905) (reprinted 1914 with Preface by ECS Wade in 1962).

[18] The author who criticized Dicey very severely was WI Jennings in *The Law and the Constitution*, 5th edn (London, University of London Press, 1959); also, 'The Report on Ministers' Powers' (1932) 10 *Public Administration* 333; and, 'In Praise of Dicey 1885-1935' (1935) 13 *Journal of Public Administration* 127.

[19] AV Dicey, 'Droit administratif in Modern French Law' (1901) 18 *Law Quarterly Review* 302–18.

to gratitude and he does not hesitate to present himself as enlightened and as resentful of criticism of the great authors of the foreign system.[20]

Dicey constructed his concept of the rule of law using three propositions:

> When we say that the supremacy of the rule of law is a characteristic of the English constitution, we generally include under one expression at least three distinct though kindred conceptions.
>
> We mean, in the first place, that no man is punishable or can be lawfully made to suffer in body or goods except for a distinct breach of law established in the ordinary legal manner before the ordinary courts of the land. In this sense the rule of law is contrasted with every system of government based on the exercise by persons in authority of wide, arbitrary, or discretionary powers of constraint.[21]
>
> We mean, in the second place, when we speak of the rule of law as a characteristic of our country, not only that with us no man is above the law, but (what is a different thing) that here every man whatever be his rank or condition, is subject to the ordinary law of the realm and amenable to the jurisdiction of the ordinary tribunals.[22]
>
> There remains yet a third and a different sense in which the 'rule of law' or the predominance of the legal spirit may be described as a special attribute of English institutions. We may say that the constitution is pervaded by the rule of law on the grounds that the general principles of the constitution (as, for example, the right to personal liberty, or the right of public meeting) are with us as the result of judicial decisions determining the rights of private persons in particular cases brought before the courts; whereas under many foreign constitutions the security (such as it is) given to the rights of the individual, results, or appears to result, from the general principles of the constitution.[23]

According to Dicey, the rule of law is one of two features which have defined England since the times of the Norman Conquest, the other being the predominance of the central power – understood as predominance of the Crown – which has now evolved in the direction of the sovereignty of Parliament.[24] If we look at the three axioms composing the rule of law according to Dicey, we can better appreciate the following principles, which he wished to stress.

First, he believed that the law – one and the same for all – needed to be decided upon by the Parliament in such a way that no sizeable margin could possibly be left to the discretion of the executive. He considered discretionary powers as arbitrariness.[25] This was easy to understand in his case, given his political ideology, because wide discretionary powers can jeopardize the will of the sovereign Parliament and can lead to the annulment de facto of the rule of law. He was especially suspicious of the French administration as – according to him – illegality was always inherent in the French public administration. He wrote: 'Royal

---

[20] AV Dicey (trs A Batut and G Jèze, Préface A Ribot), *Introduction à l'étude du droit constitutionnel* (Paris, Giard et Brière (Bibliothèque Internationale de Droit Public), 1902).

[21] Dicey, *Introduction to the Study of the Law of the Constitution*, above n 14 at 110.

[22] Ibid, 114.

[23] Ibid, 115.

[24] Ibid, 115.

[25] See the remarkable analysis on this point by Jennings in *The Law and the Constitution*, above n 18 at 306.

lawlessness was not peculiar to especially detestable monarchs such as Louis the Fifteenth: it was inherent in the French system of administration'.

In his view, wide discretionary powers constituted a danger to the rights of the citizens, and especially to their civil rights.

A characteristic of English law remained that the law must be the same for everybody. It was not admissible to have exceptions or special *regimes* for anyone. By the sixth edition of his book, we see Dicey assert that:

> If we take France as the type of continental state, we may assert, with substantial accuracy, that officials are, *or have been*, in their official capacity, *to some extent*[26] exempted from the ordinary law of the land, protected from the jurisdiction of the ordinary tribunals, and subject in certain respects only to official law administered by official bodies.[27]

In England, not only was everybody under the same legal system, but all came under the same jurisdiction, the one of ordinary justice.

The last of his axioms was that there is no rule of law in a given country, unless civil liberties are guaranteed by the ordinary courts. He did not say this directly, but it may be deduced from his analysis that he demanded a judicial protection of civil liberties. He wrote:

> But any knowledge of history suffices to show that foreign constitutionalists have, while occupied in defining rights, given insufficient attention to the absolute necessity for the provision of adequate remedies by which the rights they proclaimed might be enforced.[28]

It should be noted that, throughout his entire book, Dicey did not deal with any save two public services, the army and tax administration. Instead, he dedicated a whole chapter to defending his rule of law against the *droit administratif.* He wrote:[29]

> The historical glories of French arms conceal the important fact that, among the great States of Europe, France and England have the most constantly attempted, though with unequal success, to maintain the supremacy of the civil power against any class which defies the legitimate sovereignty of the nation.

Since the beginning, Dicey had declared that the French administrative law, the *droit administratif* – which he tended to prefer to leave untranslated – was utterly foreign to the concept of the rule of law (as proposed by him) and that therefore there was no place for it in the English legal order. Students of law must learn it, however, if only in order to be proud of their own nation.[30]

Dicey examined the notions of the *droit administratif* as delineated by a series of French authors of his time, and he found them imprecise; he complained that 'their vagueness is not without significance'. According to him, it could

---

[26] This phrase did not exist in editions one to five.
[27] Dicey, *Introduction to the Study of the Law of the Constitution*, above n 14 at 115.
[28] Ibid, 117–18.
[29] Ibid, 213–14, note 2.
[30] An excellent critical study of the contribution of AV Dicey has already been written by EM Parker, 'State and Official Liability' (1905/6) *Harvard Law Review* 335. He proves Dicey misinformed and demonstrates an excellent knowledge of the French law of his times.

be best described as that portion of French law which determines, (i.) the position and liabilities of all State officials, (ii.) the civil rights and liabilities of private individuals in their dealings with officials as representatives of the State, and (iii.) the procedure by which these rights and liabilities are enforced.[31]

Dicey was also interested in that part of the *droit administratif* known as the *contentieux administratif*, which constituted the judicial review of administrative action. In his time, and owing a great deal to the book of E Laferrière,[32] *droit administratif* and *contentieux administratif* more or less overlapped. In that sense, a legacy was left for the later development of English administrative law. In fact, the main body of any book of administrative law in modern England deals with the judicial review of administrative action, while in France, the perception of administrative law has evolved since those days. Thus judicial review of administrative action is only one of the many chapters of any book of French administrative law.

In any case, the *droit administratif* with which Dicey compared English law was not the law of 1885, the date of the first edition of his book, and still less that of 1914, when he published his last edition. He wanted to compare with the French law of the periods 1800–15 and 1830–70, because, he said, in that hypothesis alone

> we can rightly appreciate the essential opposition between our existing English rule of law and the fundamental ideas which lie at the basis of administrative law not only in France but in any country where this scheme of State or official law has obtained recognition.[33]

He considered that a comparison of the two systems, as they were developed in 1908, could lead to the conclusion that there were no essential differences in the rights of civil servants towards the citizens. Nevertheless, such a conclusion would be erroneous – according to him – as he wanted to stay, ostensibly, within the period ending with the Third Empire.

French administrative law had been – as Dicey had fully understood – reliant since its inception upon two basic principles: first, that the administration, in its relations with private individuals, did not function under the same rules as them but by a series of rights, privileges and prerogatives of its own (Dicey entirely overlooked the *gestion privée* of the state). Second, that the principle of separation of powers did not correspond to what they called, in England, the 'independence of the judiciary', but to the fact that the members of the executive needed to be independent from the judiciary and therefore exempt from the jurisdiction of the ordinary courts. In fact, Dicey ignored the specific way in which the principle of the separation of powers was conceived in France and on the continent.

According to Dicey, the following characteristics resulted from the *droit administratif*.

---

[31] Dicey, *Introduction to the Study of the Law of the Constitution*, above n 14 at 217.
[32] E Laferrière, *Traité de la juridiction administrative et des recours contentieux*, vol II (Paris, LGDJ, 1989).
[33] Dicey, *Introduction to the Study of the Law of the Constitution*, above n 14 at 217.

First, the relations between the government and its civil servants with the citizens were governed by rules which were essentially different from those ruling the relations between private individuals.

Secondly, the judiciary, the ordinary tribunals, had no jurisdiction over the relations between the state and private individuals. He noted that 'No part of revolutionary policy or sentiment was more heartily accepted by Napoleon than the conviction that the judges must never be allowed to hamper the action of the government'.[34] Dicey recognized the catastrophic intervention of the French judges in the work of the government in the *ancien régime*, yet he rejected, nonetheless, the solution provided and merely allowed his reader to read between the lines that it was the result of the despotic, tyrannical spirit of Napoleon. In his later editions he recognized the opposite:

> The incompetence, however, of the judicial courts did not mean, even under Napoleon, that a person injured by an agent of the government was without remedy. He might bring his grievance before, and obtain redress from, the administrative tribunals in substance the *Conseil d'Etat*, or proceedings might, where a crime or a wrong was complained of, be, with the permission of the government, before the ordinary courts.[35]

Thirdly, the coexistence of the two jurisdictions had resulted in conflicts of jurisdiction. The fact that originally it had been the Conseil d'Etat which had had the jurisdiction to decide on those conflicts of competence, was a matter which roused Dicey's suspicions. When the Tribunal des Conflits was created, Dicey discovered its raison d'être in its case law for administrative liability, which was to control procedures and perpetually to prolong the protection of civil servants vis-à-vis private individuals.[36] He found support for his conclusions in the pages of Léon Duguit.[37]

Fourthly, the most despotic characteristic of the *droit administratif*, was that it protected the civil servants of the state, in numerous ways, against any control from the ordinary courts. The concerns of the acts of state took precedence and came first. Dicey noted that 'of recent years the tendency of French lawyers has certainly been to narrow down the sense of an ambiguous term which lends itself easily to the justification of tyranny',[38] nonetheless, he insisted on the repercussions of the doctrine of the acts of state in the area of civil servants' responsibility. He examined Article 114 of the Penal Code which made the superior in the hierarchy responsible for the order for the execution of a crime, as well as Article 75 of the Constitution of the Year VIII, which survived up until the events of 1870, and which was abrogated by the crisis government of the times.

Finally, he declared himself absolutely certain that an Englishman would find it difficult to accept that an authority which was the first councilor to the govern-

---

[34] Ibid, 224.
[35] Ibid at 224.
[36] Ibid at 239.
[37] L Duguit and F Moreau, *Manuel de droit public français, Tome Ier, Droit constitutionnel* (Paris, 1907) 464.
[38] Dicey, *Introduction to the Study of the Law of the Constitution*, above n 14 at 226.

ment could never fail to be influenced by it, when exercising its judicial powers. He attenuated his position, however, when he wrote

> . . . administrative tribunals . . . are certainly very far indeed from being mere departments of the executive government. . . . It would therefore appear to be possible, or even probable, that droit administratif may ultimately, under the guidance of lawyers, become, through a course of evolution, as completely a branch of the law of France (even if we use the the the word "law" in its very strictest sense) as equity has for more than two centuries become an acknowledged branch of the law of England.[39]

In the final editions of his book, Dicey exalted the merits of the evolving *droit administratif.* In the meantime, the case law of the Conseil d'Etat had elaborated the distinction between *faute personnelle* and *faute de service*, while the independence of the members of the Conseil d'Etat was guaranteed. Now, he held Alexis de Tocqueville responsible for his earlier erroneous positions. However, nothing of the *droit administratif* could be imported into English law. Individual liberties were better protected in England than anywhere else in the world and – even more important – he was adamant about the supremacy of the ordinary law, applied by ordinary courts. Although the powers of the English government had been considerably increased, the *droit administratif* could not be imported to England, thanks to the characteristics of the rule of law.

Clearly, Dicey made mistakes in what related to the true nature of the French administrative law of his times, but he also made mistakes in what related to the notion of the rule of law that he proposed.

This is because he exaggerated the nature of the *droit administratif,* especially when discussing the responsibility of civil servants. It is true that, at his insistence, he was helped by the French liberals until the reforms of 1872. These had severely criticized their own national system, and Dicey cited them. The same happened a century later, on the publication of an article by Prosper Weil.[40] Dicey did not take into consideration that in French society, they always prefer to condemn the state rather than civil servants, because the state is always solvable. Hamson also commented[41] that the protection of civil liberties is not under the jurisdiction of the administrative courts in France, but remains within the remit of ordinary courts and the so-called judicial police (*police judiciaire*). Moreover, he ignored the distinction between *actes d'autorité* and *actes de gestion.*

On the other hand, nor did Dicey want to acknowledge the important changes which England and English society were undergoing in his lifetime. England was already changing rapidly before the end of the nineteenth century, leaving behind its liberal past to become an interventionist state, and making tremendous

---

[39] Dicey, *Introduction to the Study of the Law of the Constitution*, above n 14 at 251.

[40] P Weil, 'The Strength and Weakness of French Administrative Law' (1965) *Cambridge Law Journal* 242.

[41] CJ Hamson, *Executive Discretion and Judicial Control, an Aspect of the French Conseil d'Etat*, Hamlyn Lectures (London, Stevens and Sons, 1954) 72. Same observations by Parker, in his times, in 'State and Official Liability' above n 30 at 341; also, F-H Lawson, 'Dicey Revisited. I' (1959) *Political Studies* 120.

changes in the social arena. In so doing, the executive was already exercising important and wide discretionary powers. A Whig by conviction, Dicey did not want to accept this new reality.[42]

In addition to this, the famous point made by Dicey that – contrary to French law – English public administration and private individuals were under the same law could not be true. When public administration taxes, educates, provides healthcare and so on, this is because there are special laws making it possible to do it and to impose its will unilaterally on private individuals living in society. No private individual has the right to levy taxes or to raise an army, or do anything else that the English government reserves for itself, unless there is a law permitting it. It is true that there may be differences between the two systems in the area of executing the will of public powers. However, this is only in cases where the private individual concerned does not want to obey state powers; nevertheless, even this reflects the historical development of each legal system.

Furthermore, Dicey did not pay sufficient attention to a new institution – already growing rapidly during his lifetime – that of the administrative tribunals.[43] Moreover, he did not take into consideration the prerogative writs except for *habeas corpus*. From the moment that part of public administration was in the hands of the justices of peace, and there were the prerogative writs of *certiorari*, prohibition and *mandamus* against their decisions, there was an administrative law in the country, even if it was part of the common law. As there was only one jurisdiction, Dicey did not pay attention to that development. He did not understand that administrative law is the result of the specific arrangement of public administration, and not the result of the existence of a system of dual jurisdiction. This simple and clear fact was first proven by the development of American administrative law[44] and – more recently – by the rapid development of English administrative law and those of so many other Commonwealth countries.[45]

Dicey was conscious of the important developments provoked in English law by the Reform Act of 1832, with an executive full of discretionary powers, as well as of the far-reaching effects of two decisions, namely, *Board of Education v Rice* (1911)[46] and *Local Government Board v Aldridge* (1915)[47]. According to the former, any administrative decision which is not in strict conformity with the law is

---

[42] Jennings, *The Law and the Constitution*, above n 18 at 308.

[43] The typical example is WA Robson, who recognized the English administrative law in the administrative tribunals, in *Justice and Administrative Law, a Study of the British Constitution* (London, Stevens and Sons; Toronto, The Carswell Co, 1951).

[44] Among others, see JL Mashaw, *Creating the Administrative Constitution: The Lost One Hundred Years of American Administrative Law* (New Haven, Yale University Press, 2012); WC Chase, *The American Law School and the Rise of Administrative Government* (Madison WI, The Wisconsin University Press, 1982); TT Ziamou, *Rulemaking, Participation and the Limits of Public Law in the USA and Europe* (Aldershot, Ashgate, 2001); L Mayers, *The American Legal System; The Administration of Justice in the United States by Judicial, Administrative, Military, and Arbitral Tribunals* (New York, Harper and Row, 1964).

[45] The first scholar who made that observation was Jennings, *The Law and the Constitution*, above n 18 at 313.

[46] *Board of Education v Rice* (1911) AC 179.

[47] *Local Government Board v Aldridge* (1915) AC120 (F).

illegal, null and void. The second freed the administrative action from judicial procedures, asking only for a 'fair transaction of business' based on fairness and equity. Dicey noted that those developments in legislation and case law had the tendency to create something similar in essence to French administrative law. Nonetheless, he tried to save his anterior position by declaring the nature of administrative law to be irreconcilable with the English system of a unitary jurisdiction.[48]

Dicey did not understand that an expanded public administration producing decisions does not constitute per se a danger to any rule of law. It is self-evident that there is always a special group of rules only applicable to the executive, even in the most liberal and non-interventionist state. Its name is not important nor is its organization, in other words, as a distinctive body of laws, or as principles and axioms dispersed in a common law. Thus the question which needs to be answered is what remains from Dicey's rule of law and, in any case, precisely what does the rule of law mean?[49]

It cannot mean anything other than what we call state ruled by law, the submission of the executive to the law.[50] This is what remains if we remove the precarious elements from Dicey's rule of law, in particular, the confusion created by inserting elements of liberal ideology, and the peculiarities of the English judicial system. The essence of the rule of law as proposed by Dicey was simply the idea that the executive must submit to the supremacy of the law, something which can be expressed, in other words, by the sovereignty of the British Parliament and the sanction of this rule of the supremacy of the law by the judiciary.

This is the reason why Dicey saw – at the very least – no contradiction in the decision *Board of Education v Rice* if not the confirmation of his rule of law. If that was the essence of the notion of Dicey's rule of law, then it was no different whatsoever to the *principle of legality*, one of the fundamentals of French administrative law, especially in Dicey's lifetime, when French administrative law, like Dicey, was objecting to the wide discretionary powers – especially in rulemaking – of the executive.

That – in summary – is what practically remains from the rule of law in modern times. According to HWR Wade,[51] the rule of law means that the executive must

---

[48] Dicey, *Introduction to the Study of the Law of the Constitution*, above n 14 at 235 ff.

[49] No matter what the misunderstandings or erroneous positions of Dicey, he remains nonetheless the author of his times par excellence, who brought into legal discussion two points which had not attracted the attention of public lawyers before him: a) he took into consideration not only the production of the law but also its execution, b) he drew attention to the guarantees of the execution of the law in practical terms, in other words, to judicial control. P Costa, 'Lo stato di diritto: un introduzione storica' in P Costa and D Zolo (eds), *Lo stato di diritto*, above n 4 127 (the same book in English is *The Rule of Law, History, Theory and Criticism* (Springer, 2007)).

[50] This is the area where the critical contribution of Jennings becomes more important in *The Law and the Constitution*, above n 18 at 311.

[51] HWR Wade and CF Forsyth, *Administrative Law*, 10th edn (Oxford, Oxford University Press, 2009) 17; Paul Craig distinguishes between a formal and a substantive concept of the rule of law and then proceeds to discuss a third and fourth point of view in *Administrative Law*, 6th edn (London, Sweet and Maxwell, 2008); T Endicott makes an interesting approach to the issue proposing the principle of legality as a principle allied to the rule of law, in *Administrative Law*, 2nd edn (Oxford, Oxford

always act in conformity with the law and this almost always means that the executive must act with the permission of an Act of Parliament. The judiciary will not allow that those powers be used in directions other than those which were probably chosen by Parliament. An essential part of the rule of law is the prohibition of abuse of discretionary powers.

Despite his apology in the Preface of the French edition of his book, Dicey left quite a heavy legacy against French administrative law. In *Ministry of Housing and Local Government v Sharp* (1970), Lord Denning MR declared that English law does not permit civil servants to find protection behind a '*droit administratif*'.[52]

The Rule of Law or Principle of Legality in Modern Times

The principle of legality was developed by the Conseil d'Etat and its case law over centuries. As it was outlined earlier, it was a French adaptation of the English concept of the rule of law, given that the law was understood as the expression of the general will of the nation. It was in fact a very concrete expression of the political liberalism of the eighteenth century. This was because, by being submitted to the law, the executive – traditionally considered the representative of the will of the monarch – was baptized democratic. The sovereign nation, represented in the Parliament, was permitting the executive to act. In order to understand more fully the importance of this doctrinal construction, we need to remember that, within that system, the sole judge of the constitutionality of the laws was Parliament itself, that is to say, the organ enacting the law. Later, the principle of legality took on a new dimension, because it abandoned its initial ideological basis. The public administration was bound to respect not only the Acts of Parliament, but the law in general, including the rules made by the administration, because the possibility for the administration to produce legal norms was now accepted. The principle of legality became the principle of the law.[53]

In time, new sources of legality[54] for administrative action were accepted. The custom was never truly accepted in France, on the contrary, the jurisprudence of the Conseil d'Etat – and, in any case, the general principles of law as designated by the Conseil d'Etat – were considered sources of the legality of administrative

University Press, 2011) 19. Some of the best pages on these issues have been written by C Harlow and R Rawlings, in *Law and Administration*, 3rd edn (Cambridge, Cambridge University Press, 2009) 1 ff; also, P Kane, *Administrative Law*, 5th edn (Oxford, Oxford University Press, 2011) 43.

[52] *Ministry of Housing and Local Government v Sharp* [1970] 2 QB 223 at 226, [1970] 1 All ER 1009.

[53] Principe de juridicité, according to J Moreau, *Droit administratif* (Paris, PUF, 1989) 19.

[54] Flogaitis, *Les contrats administratifs*, above n 12 at 68; A de Laubadère et al, *Traité de Droit Administratif*, Tome I (Paris, LGDJ, 1994) 553; G Braibant, *Le droit administratif français*, 2nd ed (Paris, PFNSP/Dalloz, 1988) 195; R Chapus, *Droit administratif général*, vol I, 15th ed (Paris, Montchrestien, 2001); S Cassese, *Le basi del diritto amministrativo* (Torino, Einaudi, 1989) 34.

action. The general principles of law were considered in accordance with our understanding of mankind and the world, and as the expression of an ethical concept,[55] and are thus accepted as a source of legality with precedence over the autonomous decrees of Article 37 of the Constitution of 1958.[56] It is no coincidence that the jurisprudence of the Conseil d'Etat – and especially the general principles of law – was accepted as source of legality, while the doctrine was never granted that role.

The reason why the general principles of law, as developed by the Conseil d'Etat, were accepted as having such an important role in the canvas of the French legal system, was because, through them, in the new era, the Conseil d'Etat was able to incorporate system ideas and practices of the *ancien régime* and the Conseil du Roi, and thus lend them a new democratic legitimacy in a very subtle way.[57] A concrete example of this was the jurisprudence of the Conseil d'Etat according to which the ministers disposed of an autonomous power to organize and deliver public services as they wished without need of any legal provision. In modern times this has a constitutional basis in Article 37 of the French Constitution of 1958 but, up until then, its power originated historically, from the times when public administration organized itself and its functions – thanks to the fact that it represented the monarch and exercised his *jus politiae*.

The principle of legality in German law (*Prinzip der Gesetzmässigkeit*) is founded on Article 20(3) of the Fundamental Law (GG), which states that the legislative power has one limiting factor, namely the Constitution. The executive and the judicial powers are, however, bound by Acts of Parliament and the Law (*Gesetz und Recht*). Nonetheless, its true content can only really be established through the pages of history of German law. It is generally accepted that the principle of legality is composed of two sub-principles, which are the principle of the supremacy of the law (*Vorrang des Gesetzes*), and the principle of the reserve in favour of the law (*Vorbehalt des Getetzes*).[58]

---

[55] J Rivero and J Waline, *Droit administratif*, 17th edn (Paris, Dalloz, 1998) at 76.

[56] Braibant, *Le droit administratif français*, above n 47 at 211; S Rials, *Le juge administratif français et la technique du standard* (Paris, LGDJ, 1980); Y Gaudemet, *Les méthodes du juge administratif* (Paris, LGDJ, 1972); R Latournerie, 'Essai sur les méthodes juridictionnelles du Conseil d'Etat' in *Livre jubilaire pour le 150e anniversaire du Conseil d'Etat* (Paris, Sirey, 1952) 177; T Fortsakis, *Conceptualisme et empirisme en droit administratif français* (Paris, LGDJ, 1987).

[57] This simple truth appears in the writings of Alexis de Tocqueville, *L'Ancien Régime et la Révolution*, re-edited (Paris, Gallimard, 1967), but also in those of Laferrière, *Traité de la juridiction administrative et les recours contentieux*, above n 32.

[58] H-U Erichsen and W Martens, *Allgemeines Verwaltungsrecht*, 14th ed (Berlin, New York, W de Gruyter, 2010); E Forsthoff, *Lehrbuch des Verwaltungsrechts*, Band I (Allgemeiner Teil, München, Beck, 1973) 81; also, 'Die Bindung an Gesetz und Recht' (1959) *DöV* 41; also, *Rechtstaat im Wandel. Verfassungsrechtliche Abhandlungen 1950-1964* (Stuttgart, Kohlhammer, 1964) 176; E-W Böckenförde, *Gesetz und gesetzgebende Gewalt: Von den Anfängen des deutschen Staatsrechtslehre bis zur Höhe des staatsrechtlichen Positivismus* (Berlin, Duncker und Humblot, 1981) 375; M Imboden, *Das Gesetz als Garantie rechtsstaatlicher Verwaltung* (Basel, Stuttgart, Helbing und Lichtenhahn, 1954); C Gusy, 'Der Vorrang des Gesetzes' (1983) *JuS* 189; F Ossenbühl, 'Vorrang und Vorbehalt des Gesetzes' in J Isensee and P Kirchhof, *Handbuch des Staatsrechts der BRD* (Heidelberg, CF Müller, III, 1988) 315; E Schmidt-Aßmann, *Das allgemeine Verwaltungsrecht als Ordnungsidee. Grundlagen und Aufgaben der verwaltungsrechtlichen Systembildung*, 2nd edn (Berlin, Heidelberg, Springer, 2006) 43ff.

The principle of the supremacy of the law means that formal Acts of Parliament occupy a distinguished place among the sources of administrative legality. The administration must apply the Acts of Parliament, even when their content differs from the other sources of legality (*Anwendungsgebot*), as it is bound neither to deviate from them (*Abweichungsverbot*) nor to act against them.[59] The difference between this and the French concept of the principle of legality is evident: the administrative action does not always need to be based on the Acts of Parliament, it is sufficient that the administration acknowledges them and applies them either if they exist, or if their content is different from that of other sources of legality. It is, however, free to act in all other cases. This concept of the principle of legality derives from the times when absolutism evolved into constitutional monarchy. Then, the monarch was the source of all powers, a number of them were however conceded to Parliament, an expression, in those times, of the influence of the *bourgeoisie*. The monarch was therefore obliged to respect the law produced by Parliament, but free to act in all other cases.[60]

In those days of the development of the German state, both the *bourgeoisie* and the constitutional movement considered the Parliament and Acts of Parliament as the warrantors of personal freedom and private property (*Freiheit und Eigentum*) and it was intended that those areas should only be regulated by legislation produced by Parliament. This is the reason behind the inclusion of the second component of the principle of legality, the reserve in favour of the law (*Gesetzesvorbehalt*), equivalent to the reserve from attacks on personal freedom and private property (*Eingriffsvorbehalt*). This is why *Gesetzesvorbehalt* and the concept of law were well matched.[61]

In conclusion, the administrative action must never disregard the supremacy of the law compared with the other sources of legality, deviate from the law or act against it. Moreover, it cannot intervene in the sphere which is reserved for the law, in other words, the regulation of civil liberties. For all else, the public administration is free to act. It has the same freedom of action inherited from the constitutional monarch of centuries ago, and exists with its own constitutional legitimacy. In any case, administration free from the law does not mean administration free from the Constitution.

Finally, the German principle of legality has a third component, which is the principle in favour of the administration (*Verwaltungsvorbehalt*), namely, a sphere of action which is closed to the legislator as, for example, power over the

---

[59] Erichsen and Martens, *Allgemeines Verwaltungsrecht*, ibid.

[60] Ibid; Forsthoff, *Lehrbuch des Verwaltungsrechts*, above n 58 at 32; E-R Huber, *Deutsche Verfassungsgeschichte*, Band II (Stuttgart, Berlin, Köln, Kohlhammer, 1960) 16; T Oppermann, 'Gutachten C zum 51' (1976) *Deutschen Juristentag* 44.

[61] Erichsen and Martens, *Allgemeines Verwaltungsrecht*, above n 58; M Klöpfer, 'Vorbehalt des Gesetzes in Wandel' (1984) *JZ* 685; H Klein, 'Eingriffsverwaltung' (1966) *EvStL* 398; W Krebs, *Vorbehalt des Gesetzes und Grundrechte* (Berlin, Duncker und Humblot, 1975); also, 'Zum aktuellen Stand des Lehre vom Vorbehalt des Gesetzes' (1979) *Jura* 304; J Pietzcker, 'Vorrang und Vorbehalt des Gesetzes' (1979) *Jus* 710; G Kisker, 'Neue Aspekte in Streit um den Vorbehalt des Gesetzes' (1977) *Neue Juristische Wochenschrift* 1313.

administration's personnel, or its organizational power.[62] In this way, once again, the German concept of the principle of legality rejoins that of the French.

In Germany, the custom constitutes one of the sources of the principle of legality, following traditions of private law. Case law does not have the same importance as in France, especially because most of the administrative law is written law, and – since Otto Mayer's time – the doctrine continues to be an important source of inspiration. The general principles of law occupy an important place among the sources of the principle of legality. In the hierarchy of the sources they rank with legal norms from whence they derive. In many cases they serve as the perceptible evidence of constitutional rules (*Konkretisierung von Verfassungsrecht*).[63]

---

[62] P Lerche, *Übermass und Verfassungsrecht*, Köln (Berlin, München, Heymann, 1961); F Werner, 'Verwaltungsrecht als konkretisiertes Verfassungsrecht' (1959) *DVBl* 527; C-E Eberle, 'Gesetzesvorbehalt und Parlamentsvorbehalt' (1984) *DöV* 485; F Ossenbühl, *Verwaltungsvorschriften und Grundgesetz* (Bad Homburg, Berlin, Zürich, Gehlen, 1968) 214; H Heussner, 'Vorbehalt des Gesetzes und "Wesentlichkeitstheorie"' in H Avenarius et al, *Festschrift für Erwin Stein* (Bad Homburg, Gehlen, 1983) 111; D Umbach, 'Das Wesentliche an der Wesentlishkeitstheorie' in *Festschrift für HJ Haller* (München, CH Beck, 1984) 111 and 120.

[63] See F Werner, 'Verwaltungsrecht als konkretisiertes Verfassungrecht' (1959) *DVBl* 527ff.

Lesson 4

The Concept of the 'Modern' State

The term 'state' came into political and legal vocabulary together with the gradual growth of the idea of an entity, which would simultaneously be the source of its own legitimacy and the cradle of every public power that it would exercise under that name. Up to the middle of the fourteenth century, the term state meant the 'condition', or way of existing (*status reipublicae*) and it became, especially as it derived from the same cultural context as Machiavelli, the name par excellence of the territorial political organization.[1]

As we have seen, England, the country best regarded as the cradle of modern political philosophy and practice, did not produce a theory of state as a personalized entity. In terms of legal doctrine, England does not have the state as an entity, a legal body. On the contrary, some or all of England's constitutional organs are personalized and public action always refers to the organ which took it, for example, the Crown, Parliament, government, and so forth.[2] On the continent, the state is considered a legal body and all the actions taken by all the authorities in the country are ultimately taken in the name of the state.

What the authors of the nineteenth century called 'the modern state' is the result of two events, the French Revolution of 1789 and the establishment, in 1871, of the German Empire. These were extremely important political events: the first, because it was the result of a revolution which had adopted a specific doctrine, called the philosophy of the Lights, the second because it realized – for the first time – the German philosophers' dream of political union for the motherland.

As the lawyers of these two countries separated by the Rhine were serving the political philosophies and political choices made in their countries, theories which developed around the concept of state were decisively coloured by them.

---

[1] G Amato and F Clementi, *Forme di Stato e forme di governo* (Bologna, Il Mulino, 2006) 31.

[2] MS Giannini, *Il pubblico potere, Stati e amministrazioni pubbliche* (Bologna, Il Mulino, 1986).

The French Concept of State

The French Revolution followed the so-called philosophy of the Lights and, particularly, the doctrines which were advanced by Jean-Jacques Rousseau through his *Contrat social*,[3] and Montesquieu and his *De l'esprit des lois*.[4]

According to the Revolution and first Constitution, all powers belonged to the nation.[5] The French took this concept from the Greek language and tradition and transplanted it into their culture. Their ethnic heritage coloured their experience of this, however. This was because the French people were composed of a broad canvas of ethnicities and cultures, forged together by their Kings and shared centuries of struggle against the English, Spanish and German Kings and Princes. The Thirty Years' and the Hundred Years' Wars best illustrate those times. It was natural to conclude that the nation was composed of all the people living in France and having French citizenship.

The constitutions proclaimed that, essentially, sovereignty resides in the nation, thus it was concluded that the powers constituting the sovereignty of the state are those of the nation and that, therefore, the nation and the state are one and the same. The state is not an entity opposed to the nation, but personifies the nation itself, because it incorporates the powers belonging to the nation. In doing so it becomes an identical part of the nation.[6]

Consequently, the members of the nation are not third parties in relation to the state, but neither can they claim parts of the sovereignty individually. The French Revolution of 1789 proclaimed the principle of national sovereignty and the first Constitution of 1791 ruled as follows:

> The sovereignty is one, indivisible. . . It belongs to the nation; no section of the people and no individual can acquire for himself its exercise.

The nation is sovereign as a collective entity and as such is the subject of the powers constituting sovereignty, the powers of the state. Therefore it must be accepted

---

[3] J-J Rousseau, *Du contrat social et autres œuvres politiques*, Introduction de Jean Ehrard (Paris, Garnier, 1975); in English, *The Social Contract, and Discourses*, Translation and Introduction by GDHCole, JH Brumfitt and JC Hall (London, Dent, 1973); A Cobban, *Rousseau and the Modern State* (London, Allen and Unwin, 1964).

[4] Charles de Montesquieu, *De l'esprit des lois*, Edition établie par Laurent Versini (Paris, Gallimard, 1995); JN Shklar, *Montesquieu* (Oxford, Oxford University Press, 1987); DW Carrithers, MA Mosher and PA Rahe (eds), *Montesquieu's Science of Politics, Essays on the Spirit of Laws* (Lanham, Oxford, Rowman and Littlefield, 2001); I Cox, *Montesquieu and the History of French Laws* (Oxford, Voltaire Foundation, 1983).

[5] There are many studies on the state and its concept, especially of the nineteenth century, updated in all directions in the twentieth century and recent times. The most classic is R Carré de Malberg, *Contribution à la théorie générale de l'Etat, spécialement d'après les données fournies par le Droit constitutionnel français*, 2nd edn (Paris, Sirey, 1922). The author, being Professor at the University of Strasbourg, combines an excellent knowledge of the political and legal thought of the two sides of the Rhine.

[6] Ibid at 167.

as a legal body, having individual identity and a power superior and independent from the individual and individual will.

After the end of the French monarchy, the Convention changed the principle from national to people's sovereignty,[7] through the Constitution of 1793. The idea was that sovereignty resides equally in all citizens, an idea taken from Rousseau's *Contrat social*. However, this could not be accepted, especially because the electoral system was not universal and direct, but merely an electoral system based on census, and one exercised on two levels.

At the same time, the concept of sovereignty would signify a departure from the absolute character proposed by Rousseau. It would not be the absolute power of the absolutist monarch which was reversed by the Revolution, but the power exercised by each one of the organs established by the sovereign nation in order to exercise it. This was confined within the limits that the nation itself had ruled upon, through the Constitution. Léon Duguit has clarified this precept:

> In the doctrine of the national sovereignty, it's the collective person which possesses the sovereignty, and the citizens taken individually do not have even the smallest portion of it; therefore, they do not have any right to participate in the exercise of the sovereignty. The only consequence, which comes out of the national sovereignty, is that we need to find the best system to bring up the national will.[8]

In this way, national sovereignty was not to be exercised directly by the nation. The Revolution was very conservative towards the idea of letting the people directly exercise powers which were recognized as belonging to it. The Revolution's political project was the representative system.

Article 3 of the Declaration of 1789 stated that any power exercised by individuals had to emanate from the nation 'expressly', put another way, it had to have been conferred upon them by the national Constitution. Article 2 of the Preamble of Title III of the Constitution of 1791 stated that all powers emanate from the nation and no power could be exercised without 'delegation', in other words, without being delegated by the sovereign.

The delegation of powers was therefore the means for deploying the organs of the state. As the powers reside in the nation, their exercise could only be entrusted to those who would act in the name of the state. According to Article 3 of the same Constitution, the legislative power was delegated to the National Assembly, the executive power was delegated to the King, and the judicial power was delegated to the judges.

This idea of delegation led to the principle of representation, and Article 2 of the same Constitution stated that the French Constitution was based on representation. All those who exercised state powers did so only because they were representatives of the nation, which had delegated to them the powers, they exercised. Although this is true for all those exercising public power, and this is also part of the wider concept of representation, there is another, more restricted concept of

---

[7] Ibid at 152.
[8] L Duguit, *Traité de droit constitutionnel*, 3rd edn (Paris, Sirey, Paris, E de Boccard, I, 1927) 436.

representation, intended only for the representation of the nation in the National Assembly through elections. The Revolution had created a system in the name of the nation, in which – ironically – it did not truly trust. The nation should act through representatives in the National Assembly, who would act in the name of the nation but without an imperative mandate, that is to say, without the electoral body being able to dictate specific and detailed political decisions. This stood in conflict with all Rousseau's theories; he wanted the members of the National Assembly to be commissaries of the people, rather than mere representatives.[9]

The French Revolution abolished a hereditary monarchy, which was closely linked, historically, to the existence and concept of France, a monarchy of an absolutist state, where the phrase of King Louis XIV *'L'Etat c'est moi'* was not far from the truth. They needed to replace that form of sovereignty with another, the sovereignty of all citizens unified together, the nation. When the King reacted by fleeing, his execution only helped to establish this new concept of sovereignty.

Unity of the sovereign and unity of the state were very important for the Revolution; that unity would be helped by the unity of the law. For the first time in France, the same law should apply to all; that unity of law would be helped by a centralized, monolithic, hierarchical public administration, which would guarantee that the law would truly be applied equally to all. Decentralization could have meant differentiation in the way the law was applied in different places and the principle of equality of all before the law could thus have been in jeopardy.[10]

In fact, what the Revolution wanted to achieve was the creation of a common market in the hexagon, where the same rules would apply everywhere and industry, trade and commerce would not find obstacles in the form of privileges and exceptions. The unity of the law and state also imposed the abolition of all internal frontiers, boundaries and customs which were common all over pre-revolutionary France. It was, in a sense, a pre-figuring of what happened in Europe under different conditions and at a different pace after the Second World War.

The German Concept of State

The German theory of state is different from that of her neighbours, mainly because the political background of the societies composing the German nation produced marked differences. Germany before 1871 was a territory claimed in the name of the German nation, but was one ruled by many and various Kings and Princes. This was chiefly the result of the Thirty Years' War which had taken place on German soil and finally imposed upon the Germans numerous political divisions and many small states. The unifying element of those societies were the

---

[9] Carré de Malberg, *Contribution à la théorie générale de l'Etat*, above n 5 at 175.
[10] S Flogaitis, *La notion de décentralisation en France, en Allemagne et en Italie* (Paris, LGDJ, 1979).

language, culture and the feeling that they adhered to the same system of values but also of blood, in other words, to the same nation.

Therefore, in Germany, the word 'nation' did not have the same meaning as in France. The nation was not composed of all the citizens of the state, because the unifying element of a state did not exist; the nation pre-existed the states composing the political canvas of the ancestral German territory, scattered as it was across many states. It effectively requested political unity in its own name. As there were Germans and German communities both in ancestral central German lands, but also in many others scattered all over Central and Eastern Europe up to the Volga river, the dream of unity of the German nation around a state would have consequences of all sorts in the decades to come.

In the nineteenth century, Prussia was able to impose its own concept of a unified German state on the rest of the states of the German territory, and achieved this, strangely enough, through the Prussian–French war, which led to the creation of the German Empire and its Constitution of 1871.

In the meantime, the ascending German *bourgeoisie* was flirting with some of the ideas coming from France and with notions of political liberalism coming from England. However, the so-called German constitutional movement did not produce a true revolution; the constitutional movement led to the so-called Frankfurt Parliament and the Constitution of 1848, which remained unsuccessful because of the unwillingness of various states to give up their sovereignty.

The *bourgeoisie* compromised with the state, shaped as it was with historical influences and representing mainly the feudal aristocracy around the Emperor. They were called 'the society' (*Gesellschaft*) and were recognized as the antipodes of the state. The political theory and practice was built on the idea of a continuous struggle between state and society, two realities well-distinguished from each other. The state of the old aristocracy was located with the King and public administration, whilst the society was represented and expressed by Parliament, especially for the defence of civil rights against any possible attempt to challenge from the state.[11]

This reform process was organized by the state itself – from above, as they still say today in Germany – around the ideas expressed by various thinkers, but mainly those presented by Freiherr vom Stein, an intellectual and reformer, in his *Nassauer Denkschrift* of 1807. Vom Stein wanted gradually to draw the *bourgeoisie* into all levels of the public life within the framework of a constitutional monarchy. In this way, he hoped to achieve the political transformation of the country without the potential violent and uncontrolled destruction of pre-existing structures.[12]

---

[11] There are many books and contributions written on this issue, see, as an introduction to them, Flogaitis, *La notion de décentralisation*, ibid; also, E Forsthoff, *Deutsche Verfassungsgeschichte der Neuzeit*, 4th edn (Stuttgart, Kohlhammer, 1972).

[12] 'Every municipality has, following para. 184 of the Constitution of the Reich of 1848, as its fundamental constitutional right, the autonomous administration of the municipal affairs, including the local police, under the state tutelage organized by the law', W von Blume, *Über deutsche Selbstverwaltung* (Universität Tübingen, Rede des Rektors am Geburtstag des Königs, 1917), (Tübingen, Mohr (P Siebeck), 1917) 10.

At the beginning of the nineteenth century, the *bourgeois* movement was burgeoning under the impulse of French philosophy and demanding increased participation in the political direction of the country. This situation was reflected on a political and philosophical level by the differentiation and opposition between state and society. It should be stressed that the *bourgeoisie* wanted that power for itself, identifying itself with the society, as they were the only ones to have the *status activus*, others being under their protection (*Schutzverwandten*).[13]

These ideas were mainly promoted by the constitutionalists of the South but they found direct expression mainly in the sociological writings of Lorenz von Stein.[14] The central point of his theories was that there is a community of individuals – the society – which, independent as it is from the state, is also opposed to it and limits it. State and society operate separately although they interfere with each other, with resulting tensions. The status of the state is above that of the society and it ensures that all are equal before the law; it is therefore a state of law (*Rechtsstaat*) but, at the same time, it is a social state (*sozialer Staat*),[15] having among its aims the promotion of the economic and social progress of its members.[16]

It was during this period of transition, and consequently of tensions between the feudal heritage and an ascending *bourgeoisie*, that the theories of state were elaborated upon by German lawyers. It should also be noted that in German state philosophy, the social state was affirmed early on. As the central state was in the hands of the old aristocracy, this could be interpreted as owing a debt to the years when the feudal overlords were obliged to take care of their people.

The second challenge for the German public lawyers of the nineteenth century was that the Constitution of 1871 – the first ever to realize dreams of German unity – had expressly recognized the components of the Reich as states. It was the first time that European legal thinking was facing a situation where components of the state were already states themselves. The idea of unity as a main characteristic of the state, the idea that the state monopolizes public power, were contradicted by the Constitution itself. A further complication was that, since the French Revolution, it had become a commonly accepted principle that the state existed, because the Constitution required it within the limits it prescribed. A solution was

---

[13] O Gönnenwein, *Gemeinderecht* (Tübingen, Mohr (P Siebeck), 1963) 13.

[14] As distinguished from Freiherr vom Stein. See eg L von Stein, Verwaltungslehre, vol 8 (Stuttgart, Scientia Verlag, 1865–1884); *Geschichte der sozialen Bewegung in Frankreich von 1789 bis auf unsere Tage* (Leipzig, Otto Wigand, 1850).

[15] For the importance of Lorenz von Stein's contribution in the development of the concept of the social state, see mainly EW Bökenförde, 'Lorenz von Stein als Theoretiker der Bewegung von Staat und Gesellschaft zum Sozialstaat' in *Recht, Staat, Freiheit: Studien zur Rechtsphilosophie, Staatstheorie und Verfassungsgeschichte* (Frankfurt am Main, Suhrkamp, 1991) 170.

[16] 'The biggest part of the scientific work of Lorenz von Stein applies to a specific period of the evolution of the liberal and monarchical State. It is based on the dialectical opposition between the equality of the citizens and the social inequality in a given moment of the technical and economic evolution', E Forsthoff, *Lehrbuch des Verwaltungsrechts*, I, Allgemeiner Teil, 10th edn (München, Beck, 1973) 471. The author who introduced that approach of the German state to the French speaking world was N Poulantzas, in *Pouvoir politique et classes sociales* (Paris, Maspero, 1972).

needed, and it would be found through a new reading of the concept of state and its characteristics.

In Germany it was not the political philosophers or the statesmen who would propose the concept of the state, or of the 'modern' state, as they called it in order to reflect the new political realities. Instead, it was the professors of law, who fulfilled this role, they included CFV Gerber,[17] Paul Laband,[18] Georg Jellinek[19] and his son Walter Jellinek,[20] and others. The proposed concept would accommodate German political needs, but it would also concurrently accommodate the needs of every other state of the world. It would prove more exportable than the French one, because it was politically neutral – in terms of the form of government. Ironically, it was also accommodating many other emerging nations. In fact, the French concept of nation requires a pre-existing society composed within the boundaries of a given state. By contrast, the German concept was useful to nations trying to affirm themselves against empires through revolutions which aimed to create national states.

According to the German model, at the beginning, there needed to be a community of people which shared the same interests and which aimed to serve those interests via the creation of a state. Through the common will of everyone, this gave rise to the state, an institution, which, although created by the people, did not clash with their community and which stood alone in its own right. It was intended to be a territorial institution of public law, which did not depend on others and which unilaterally produced the law ruling everyone living in the territory of the given state.[21]

By their collective will, the people themselves gave rise to the state, but immediately after that, it became purely an organ of it, as were several others. The Constitution was the document which organized the state and its powers, especially the status of its various organs, both direct and indirect. The direct organs were those which had not been designated by another organ, for example, the people. Direct organs may have given rise to other, indirect ones, for example, the people elected Parliament, an indirect organ of the state. This model did not allow room for the French theory of delegation of powers by the nation to others; the Parliament was not delegated but designated by the people. Furthermore, as the power resided in the state, everybody else served the state and its purposes as one of its organs.

This is the organic theory of the state, which allows room for a monarch – if there is one – or for the people. As soon as the state is created, however, the people

---

[17] CFV Gerber, *Grundzüge eines Systems des deutschen Staatsrechts* (Leipzig, B Tauschnitz, 1865).

[18] P Laband, *Das Staatsrecht des deutschen Reiches*, 4th edn (Tübingen, Mohr (P Siebeck), 1911–13).

[19] G Jellinek, *Allgemeine Staatslehre* (Kronberg, Athenaeum, 1976) (reprinted from the 3rd edn of 1913).

[20] W Jellinek, *Verwaltungsrecht* (Berlin/Zürich, Gehlen, 1966) (reproduction from the 3rd edn of 1931).

[21] Apart from the above-mentioned authors, excellent commentary was also written by H Rosin, 'Souveränität, Staat, Gemeinde, Selbstvewaltung' in *Annalen des deutschen Reiches für Gesetzgebung, Verwaltung und Statistik* (München/Leipzig, Hirth, 1883).

lose their sovereignty in favour of the state. There is also a place for all sorts of regimes, including fascism and totalitarianism. In any case, in this concept of state, the monarch has his position as one of its direct organs, as he has not been elected by anyone, and the people, the *bourgeoisie*, the *Gesellshaft*, have their own position, again, because these are not elected by anyone.

The character of the German states which composed the Reich required a great deal of consideration and effort from German public law, because the concept of sovereignty – a core characteristic of every state – had to be reconceived.

Paul Laband started exploring this issue, but it was Georg Jellinek who provided the most satisfactory answer which was that the characteristic of the state is not sovereignty as conceived at the beginning, but the condition of not being bound but by its own will. When a state cannot be bound except by its own will, then it is sovereign. On the other hand, local government entities are bound by a will which is superior to theirs. As stated by Jellinek, the concept of sovereign state has only a historical value: in the past, sovereignty could be seen as an essential element of the state, but this is no longer the case.[22] The true characteristic of the state is to create the rules by which it governs by itself, and from its own will to do so, and thus organize itself. Therefore, the Member State of a federation is a true state because it is self-organized, produces its own legislation, has its own administration and operates its own system of justice. This doctrine was accepted everywhere in continental Europe, including France.

---

[22] Jellinek, *Allgemeine Staatslehre*, above n 19 at 475.

Lesson 5

From Decentralization to Devolution

The French concept of decentralization and the recent devolution of powers in Great Britain are ideologically removed from each other by quite some distance. All concepts pertaining to the organization of public powers constitute important aspects of state organization and reflect mentalities and doctrines characteristic of nations which evolve with time.

Decentralization

The state born out of the French Revolution of 1789 was meant to be centralized. According to the political doctrine known as Jacobinism, equality before the law was only guaranteed through the centralization of public administration. This was because it was thought that, in order to achieve genuine equality, the law must be applied by the same person for all as the best means of guaranteeing that he applies the law in the same way in all cases. In a decentralized system of public administration, there is a multiplicity of individuals around the country who are called upon to apply the legislation of a specific area: consequently they run the risk that every one of them will understand and apply the law slightly differently.

The terms 'concentration' and its opposite, 'de-concentration' and those of 'centralization' as opposed to 'decentralization' were proposed by the political philosophy and public law of those times of revolution; they live on, and continue to be in use in modern French administrative law.

Concentration and de-concentration constitute a binomial which describes two organizational schemes within one and the same administrative organization. Concentration is the organizational scheme where all decisive powers are in the hands of central organs. Conversely, de-concentration is the organizational scheme where all the decisive powers are given to non-central organs, again, within one and the same administration.

The binomial centralization–decentralization describes the organizational schemes which are developed in the relations between two public bodies, especially between the administration of the state and other public bodies, such as the municipalities. These have their own legal character because, under the French tradition of centralized public administration and state, the other public administrative bodies are perceived as being detached from the state.

The new states did not dissolve the municipalities; they conserved them, first because they needed them to deal with local issues, but also because they were preserving traditions in the new era, such as their own forms of government, practices and so on. In countries such as Italy for centuries several communes had already existed as real states, with large territories and enjoying international influence. As the new state arose, it compromised with them in numerous ways. However, as a general rule, the communes – no matter how old they were – had to be entirely subject to the power of the states and had to acquire new rules of organization and action, as prescribed by the law. Even when old privileges were maintained or respected, it was by the will of the state and its law.

England was, once more, the country exporting its political ideas about decentralization. This time it influenced Germany, and not France, as was the case of the representative system of government.

In the eighteenth and the nineteenth centuries, the political system known as self-government had taken shape in England. There, local government consisted of the organization of boroughs and counties throughout the country. The special feature of this organization – from the point of view of a continental lawyer[1] – is that the central administration around the Crown reserved foreign policy for itself, as well as matters pertaining to the currency, army, taxation, customs and the system of central justice. Every other activity – normative, administrative and jurisdictional – remained within the competence of the boroughs and counties. These developed their own machineries, administration, taxes, rulemaking and their activities which they were keen to develop; they had *every* competence, even without specific parliamentary provision, on the condition that none would be among those foreseen by law for the government. That was the core concept of local government, composed by organs of the Crown having legal personality of their own.[2] That system was much admired on the continent, but was rarely understood.[3]

The political philosophy of France, underpinning her arrangements for local government, was influenced by the writings of Alexis de Tocqueville who – full of admiration for the United States of America – described, in his book, *De la démocratie en Amérique*,[4] the institutions and virtues of the new country and put a lot of emphasis on American local institutions and their importance. He is the

---

[1] This is a pertinent observation of MS Giannini, *Il pubblico potere, Stati e amministrazioni pubbliche* (Bologna, Il Mulino, 1986).

[2] The Law of local government continues to be a special subject of study in the United Kingdom, outside the manuals of administrative law.

[3] England and the British Empire have introduced practical solutions to very specific problems with no equal: one of these was the way in which the British Empire infiltrated and ruled the Indian subcontinent for centuries, through the institution known as the Honourable East India Company. It was established by Royal Charter by Queen Elizabeth I in 1600, and as from 1707, was the British Joint-Stock Company. In 1773, the Company started exercising governmental powers, which continued until the passing of the Government of India Act 1858, when the British Government took direct control of the so-called British Raj.

[4] A de Tocqueville, *De la démocratie en Amérique*, new edn (Paris, Gallimard, 1968); also, *L'Ancien régime et la Révolution*, new edn (Paris, Gallimard, 1967).

originator of the idea that there is a distinction between general and local interests, the first belonging to the state and the second entrusted to local communities. The distinction between general and local interests as the basis of the distribution of power in any state has not lost its importance, even today.[5]

The state, as created by the French Revolution, needed to resolve the issue of the status of the municipalities. These were entities of territorial organization which were much older than the states themselves. The French Revolution and the state that it created were *completely* centralized and very suspicious of any other territorial power which could potentially antagonize them.

This is the reason why the local authorities which existed in post-revolutionary France were called 'decentralized', a word having nothing in common with local autonomies and which also implied that local authorities were part of the unified state. For years, the true legal status and character of the local authorities remained unclear in the minds of French public lawyers, because it was difficult to reconcile the idea that there were other territorial public entities exercising public power over the citizens of the territory of the state. Finally, it was accepted that if the local authorities pre-existed the state in their sociological form, in the modern state they existed because they were required by it. By law, this kind of symbiosis described their status and competences.[6]

The law prohibited the local authorities from having any political role; they could only be part of the administration, their acts and the status of their authorities, council and mayoral elections all under the control of the state. These were understood not as political but rather as administrative procedure. As M Hauriou explained:[7] 'The decentralization is a way of existence of the State, characterized by the fact that the State is reorganized in a certain number of administrative persons'.

On the other hand, there was a steady increase in recognizing and granting more autonomy to the decentralized entities, or communes. This movement generally included the so-called intermediary bodies; they were meant to include all those associations, groupings and initiatives – to name but a few – operating in society. In other words, the state should not control everything, but some things – as sizeable and significant as possible – should be left to the organization of society.[8] The main impetus behind this movement was the Catholic Church, which

---

[5] Despite the fact that it is out of date. It is more than obvious that this distinction, coming out of the agricultural era, can no longer be the basis of any distribution of power, because in our times there is no local interest which cannot quickly become national, just as there is no national interest which does not have a local reference. See, in detail, S Flogaitis, *La notion de décentralisation en France, en Allemagne et en Italie* (Paris, LGDJ, 1979).

[6] Flogaitis, ibid.

[7] M Hauriou, *Etude sur la décentralisation, Extrait du Répertoire du droit administratif* (Paris, P Dupont, 1892) 37.

[8] This point of view was mainly proposed within the framework of the so-called theory of the institution; the French professor M Hauriou is the best-known representative of that theory in Europe, but perhaps the best of all was the Italian professor Santi Romano, pupil of the founder of Italian administrative law, Vittorio Emmanuele Orlando, and master of Massimo Severo Giannini. See, in particular, S Cassese, *Tre maestri di diritto pubblico* (Università degli Studi Suor Orsola Benincasa, Facoltà di Giurisprudenza, Editoriale Scientifica, 2012).

had suddenly lost its position of importance on the institutional canvas of France as well as in other countries which were adopting French ideas for a modern state.

Selbstverwaltung

Even more important was that the liberals of the continent were looking to England and English local government and trying to import English self-government to continental Europe. The most important attempts were made by the Germans because – according to the reform strategy of the state – the state should remain in the hands of the old society, the aristocracy of feudal times, but there should also be an important system of local authorities to be entrusted to the 'society', the ascending *bourgeoisie*. This way, the new society would pass through a learning process as to how public powers are organized and should be exercised so that – in due time – it, too, would be ready to participate in state affairs.

In the late nineteenth century, Otto von Gierke and Hugo Preuss developed a theory of state, which was trying to explain and to consolidate into one, the state and the municipalities.[9]

According to both of these members of the German historical school of institutions (*germanische rechtsgeschichtliche Forschung*) there is a German spirit for creating communities (*Genossenschaften*). Such communities have their own organization and are recognized as legal entities of corporative character (*Korporation* or *Körperschaft*). They are gradually incorporated among them (*Stufenbau*) and have the state as the supreme instance of this social model; the state is an association of the other sub-state corporations. In Gierke's parlance, it is an organized village (*Der Staat ist das organisierte Dorf*). However, it has a certain quality which puts it beyond the other corporations, and this is called the supreme commandment (*Herrschaft*). Through this, the state is separated from the society (*staatsbürgerliche Gesellschaft*) and exists in opposition to it, because the society cannot ask for more than civil liberties and legally-protected participation.

---

[9] H Preuss, *Gemeinde, Staat, Reich als Gebietskörperschaften, Versuch einer deutschen Staatskonstruktion auf Grundlage der Genossenschaftstheorie* (Berlin, Springer, 1889); also, *Staat und Stadt, Vortrag gehalten in der Gehe-Stiftung zu Dresden am 7. November 1908 in Berlin* (Leipzig, Teubner, 1909); also, *Das städtische Amtsrecht in Preussen* (Berlin, Reimer, 1902); also, 'Die Entwicklung der kommunalen Selbstverwaltung in Deutschland' in G Anschütz, F Berolzheimer, G Jellinek, M Lenz et al (eds), *Handbuch der Politik*, vol I, *Die Grundlagen der Politik* (Berlin und Leipzig, Rothschild, 1920) 186–266; 'Selbstverwaltung, Gemeinde, Staat, Souveränität' in *Staatsrechtliche Abhandlungen, Festgabe für P Laband*, II (Tübingen, Mohr (P Siebeck), 1908); O von Gierke, *Das deutsche Genossenschaftsrecht*, vol I, *Rechtsgeschichte der deutschen Genossenschaft* (Berlin, Weidmann, 1868); also, *Deutsches Privatrecht*, vol I, *Allgemeiner Teil und Personnenrecht* (Leipzig, Duncker und Humblot, 1895) in von K Binding (ed), *Systematisches Handbuch der deutschen Wissenschaft*, Zweite Abteilung, dritter Teil, erster Band; also, *Die Steinsche Städteordnung, Rede zur Feier des Geburtstages Seiner Majestät des Kaisers und Königs gehalten in der Aula der Universität zu Berlin am 27. Januar 1909* (Berlin, Schade (O Francke), 1909).

Gierke was influenced by the doctrines of Hegel, a propos of the supreme eminence and universal nature of the state. Consequently, although he tried to propose a communitarian model of state structure, ultimately he concluded that the state needed to be respected for its *Herrschaft*, which pre-existed communitarian society.

Hugo Preuss also tried to circumvent the difficulties inherent in the theory of Gierke. He proposed a concept of state, based entirely on communities and created by them. According to him, the state was a mere association of associations, each one of which had its own structure, as well as legislative, administrative and jurisdictional functions. He negates the eminence of state sovereignty and he believes that, if the political realities of his country do not correspond to his conception of state, this is because of the survival of absolutism, which he expects to disappear gradually, following the advancement of the new model based on communities.

Such theories are interesting for lawyers of the modern day because they help us to understand how the Germans were trying to exalt the virtues of the nascent nation and marry a modern approach to the state with national mythology. However, the internal political compromises of the new state needed an immediate reform of local administration, because the communes were to be left at the political responsibility of the *bourgeoisie*. This reform needed inspiration behind it and scholars to prepare it. That work was done by Rudolf von Gneist.[10]

Instead of looking to German sources and thereby reflecting the German mentality, Rudolf von Gneist, found inspiration from English practices of self-government. Through his writings, Germany and the whole of Europe, learned of and admired the workings of English self-government. The truth is, however, that what they learned was a German reading of English self-government, serving very specific German national political needs.

In view of his study of English self-government, Gneist wrote that *Selbstverwaltung* (self-administration) was the administration of the district (*Kreis*) and the commune (*Ortsgemeinde*) according to the law of the country (*Land*), by administrators who were not professionals (*Ehrenämter*) of either middle or upper level, on the basis of taxes levied on the people living in the community.

Self-administration was an intermediate construction (*Zwischenbau*) between the state and society and aimed to bring them unity. Gneist also understood the function of self-administration as an educational process, particularly as a means of educating the new society in the affairs of state because – this way – the people (*Volk*) would gradually obtain political freedom (*zur Freiheit*).

---

[10] *Das heutige englische Verfassungs- und Verwaltungsrecht* (Berlin, Springer, 1892), vol I: *Geschichte und heutige Gestalt der Ämter in England* (1857); vol II: *Die heutige englische Kommunalverfassung und Kommunalverwaltung* (1960); vol III: *Die Geschichte des Self-government in England* (1862); also, *Self-government, Kommunalverfassung und Verwaltungsgeschichte in England*, 3rd edn (Berlin, Springer, 1871); also, *Der Rechtstaat und die Verwaltungsgerichte in Deutschland*, 2nd edn (Berlin, Springer, 1879).

Gneist professed that self-administration was a local state administration, exercised by non-professionals, in other words, by representatives of the *bourgeoisie*. He transcribed the fact that the English boroughs and counties were personified organs of the Crown into having German local authorities as *organs* of the state; the misinterpretation is self-evident as is its political background.

Gneist's theories played a considerable role in the administrative reforms of his country in 1870. Through the turbulent years of German political history, they led to the modern concept of the *Selbstverwaltung* as an indirect administration of the state (*mittelbare Staatsverwaltung*).[11]

From Federalism to Regionalism

The United States of America was the first country of federal character. The idea was that several independent states got together and produced a new state, a federal state, and the only one which would be internationally sovereign. The federated states would keep their character as states, but they abdicated international sovereignty once and for all. The expression of the common will took the form of a Constitution, distributing powers between the federal state and the states composing it. A civil war ensured that this was truly the concept on which the United States of America resided.

That new idea migrated and was introduced in Europe through the experiment of the Constitution of the German Empire of 1871. It was repeated in the Fundamental Law of Bonn (*Grundgesetz*) of 1949, where the *Länder* – as recomposed after the Second World War – were becoming part of the new federal state. This time, however, the situation was not as clear-cut as in the American case. First, this was because the German states did not remain within the German Empire of their own will. A second reason was because the *Länder* of the post-war period had not existed in the immediate past, inter alia, because they had lost their state character during the Nazi period.

Moreover, the Federal Republic of Germany had one Civil Code, one Commercial Code, one Criminal Law, one Civil Procedure, one Criminal Procedure, one Administrative Procedure Act and so on. The question remained as to what, among the important expressions of statehood, was left outside the unitary state.

The Republic of Italy brought its own new concept to Europe, that of the regions; they would include both those of extraordinary and of ordinary character, the former being introduced as an immediate response to the threat of the territorial disintegration of the state, whilst the latter developed as part of the normal way of organizing the Republic.

---

[11] W Weber, *Die Körperschaften, Anstalten und Stiftungen des öffentlichen Rechts. Eine rechtstechnische Untersuchung ihrer gegenwärtigen Ordnung* (München/Berlin, Beck, 1940); also, *Staats- und Selbstverwaltung in der Gegenwart* (Göttingen, Schwartz, 1953); and extensive bibliography since.

For a long period of time, the Italian public law was not able precisely to interpret what the regions – as described in the Constitution of 1947 – were. Ultimately, it was accepted that their rules reflected the character of law and, specifically, that of regional law. This was something of a novelty, given that the law was traditionally seen as the expression of the general will and not of the will of a territorial entity. In this way, the regions were understood as political entities and it was said that what differentiated them from the federated states was that the regions were created by the state through the Constitution, while the federated states create the state themselves.[12]

It was quickly realized that this was a fiction, especially if the Italian regions were compared with the German *Länder*. The truth was that, through the Italian Constitution of 1947, both the Republic as well as the regions were created simultaneously, by the will of the people of Italy. The state existed in as much the regions did, and vice versa: the new state was organized in two levels, with separate powers kept for the Republic and for the regions. Each one of them was responsible in its own capacity as a territorial political organization.[13]

The Spanish Constitution of 1978 went even further by creating autonomous provinces with wide powers, political force and autonomy. This just stopped short of international representation. Once more, the disintegration of the state was facilitated through the Constitution, which built the foundation of this distribution of power in the same way and via the same principle as in Italy.

States created by international intervention to accommodate difficult coexisting populations – such as Bosnia and Herzegovina – constitute even more extreme examples because the distribution of power is based on international treaty.[14]

Brazil, India and others are examples of the inadequacy of old concepts about federal and regional states. The criterion initially proposed is of no importance, unless a right of secession were to be recognized to the federated states.

The interesting feature of this internal evolution of states is that public international law has not yet taken sufficient note of it. According to that law, international liability is only of concern to the states and not to sub-state entities. This is an anachronism when the state cannot, under the Constitution, control the way sub-state entities exercise their powers. It is time for international representation

[12] The discussion was rich and fruitful in the 1950s, 1960s and 1970s, with excellent contributions from the Italian public lawyers. See the account of this discussion in Flogaitis, *La notion de décentralisation en France, en Allemagne et en Italie*, above n 5.

[13] This is an observation made by MS Giannini and it is true in its simplicity and clarity. The traditional legal doctrine has not taken note of this simple truth, mainly because it always remains true that the nation can change it – through the amendment procedure of the Constitution – and come back to the classic unitary state. Nonetheless, the political realities, as well as the constitutional canvas of regionally-organized countries, do not truly justify those considerations. The constitutions must be read as living documents; their institutions are interrelated in a dynamic way.

[14] This is an interesting development, needing more attention. There have been cases in the past where the Constitution of a country was mandated by international conferences if not directly part of an international treaty. In recent times, however, with the internationalization of intra-state developments, we see more and more evidence of the presence of the international factor in the daily life of states. The creation of combined national–international membership national courts is another example of the same development.

and international liability to be distinguished from each other, or be reconsidered with variations in order to respond to cases like this. As those sub-state entities (exercising their constitutional powers in their own name) are responsible for their decisions and actions within the state, they should equally be responsible internationally, insofar as the state can neither influence nor prevent them.

Devolution

What British politicians and public lawyers call devolution is another example of the breaking-down of states, once again evidencing the ingenuity of the old Albion.

Devolution is the specific political and legal action which characterized the passing of power from the central constitutional organs of the United Kingdom to those created in Scotland, Wales and Northern Ireland, in terms of lawmaking, political direction and administration. The transfer of power from the centre to the periphery is not a novelty, especially in the modern world. The way this was realized in the United Kingdom nonetheless constituted a novelty, evidence of the creative way of facilitating politics through conventions in that country.

The core element of devolution is that it has been decided upon and designed by Acts of Parliament, that is to say that, from the point of view of a continental lawyer, by legal instruments which are both easily and centrally changeable. Those Acts of Parliament are accompanied by a series of memoranda of understanding, as well as concordats, in other words political agreements, which have no precedent for a unitary state. This means that the whole operation is based on political agreement among political forces of a given moment in time. These have been partially translated into legislation, while the Supreme Court has been called upon to be the warrantor of the new legal architecture of the country. In the absence of that necessary guarantee, the political structure and function of this country would, once again, be guaranteed by conventions rather than by legal rules.

Devolution in the United Kingdom is an excellent example of how Great Britain continues being innovative and uses a flexible system of government. It is also the best example of a new era into which the states are entering. From the times of the American Constitution and through the introduction of the concept of federal government, the world has arrived at the regionalization of public powers through new constitutions or amendments of pre-existing ones, and to pseudo-federal states. Devolution demonstrates that a state can be reconfigured into new component parts without going through the constitutional formalities of former times.

Lesson 6

The 'Modern' State: From the One-class State to the Multi-class State[1] and its Evolution

The absolutist state was an interventionist state. With the adoption, in the widest terms, of the principle of general interest, it intervened in economic life, acquired property – both public and private – and created economic activities of all sorts. In addition, it introduced some of the best-known pieces of art with which to decorate and augment the cities, established universities and promoted a variety of public interventions in the everyday life of its citizens in order to improve all sectors, such as health and education. In short, it is no coincidence that monarchs of the absolutist state have remained and shone in cultural memory as the illuminated absolutist monarchs.[2]

The French Revolution then changed everything. The state that it introduced was – institutionally-speaking – in the hands of one class, namely, the *bourgeoisie*.

The One-class State of the Nineteenth Century

The French Revolution changed the concept of state, because it proclaimed the sovereignty of the nation. It was the first time that the state had had a legitimacy not based on the persona of the monarch and his personal claim of entitlement to power, but one based on the entire population. In spite of the doctrinal differences between the French and German concepts of state, it was accepted all over Europe that the power which generates the creation of states is the people, who are, collectively, personified in the state, according to the French doctrine. Alternatively, they may collectively create the state and once that state is created,

---

[1] This terminology was introduced by MS Giannini in his various writings, bringing elements from the social sciences into legal language. The idea was, of course, shared by many social scientists, especially in the period after the Second World War. It is useful in the sense that it is an interpretation tool for understanding institutions and mechanisms of power.

[2] Also exposed by MS Giannini, *Il pubblico potere, Stati e amministrazioni pubbliche* (Bologna, Il Mulino, 1986) 31ff. See also, G Poggi, *Lo Stato: natura, sviluppo, prospettive* (Bologna, Il Mulino, 1992) 83, (ch 3, 'Lo sviluppo dello stato moderno', II).

the people become one of its direct organs.[3] Thus, for the first time, the democratic principle became the basis of the state.

This way, the new state was built and developed on two main foundations, what would be called the electorate, and the public administration.

Nowhere in any of the proposed models of state in those days, were the people called upon to take decisions according to the principles of direct democracy. On the contrary, they could only express their opinions through proclaimed elections, by their representatives. As stated in the French Constitution of 1791, this practice established a representative democracy.

The French Revolution was the result of thinkers and political activists who were thinking and acting in the name of, and for the interests of, the people, but not with the people. It was the result of a group of revolutionaries who believed that societies, although the force creating states, should entrust their future to the elite, to the chosen ones, namely, the avant-garde. The people would only act through their representatives, who would be elected without imperative mandate.[4]

The idea of representation was, yet again, an English import. France had its own tradition of representation with the Etats-généraux, a Parliament which was occasionally called upon by the King and composed of representatives of the three classes of the society – the aristocrats, the clergy and the *bourgeoisie* and others. This happened in order to discuss the issues of the realm with imperative mandate, in other words, every member of it should act according to the directions given to him by his electorate in the so-called *cahiers de charge*.

The Etats-généraux, convened by the last King, with the driving force of the Third Estate, promoted the Revolution by proclaiming themselves in Parliament alongside the new features of governance. Each member of that Parliament would not be bound by directions given to him by his electorate, but he would – instead – represent the nation as a whole.

In those times, the idea of representation brought over from England did not have much in common with the concept of national representation. Originally, in England, Members of Parliament represented specific constituencies, which could not be classed as territorial units as, for example, the universities of Oxford or Cambridge.

Sovereignty belonged to the nation and, from that time forward, modern states would be created on the basis of that principle. The Crown had to be accommodated in the new entity – the state – in the role of the head of state, in other words, as one of the direct organs of the state, with limited powers, in accordance with what was prescribed by the Constitution.

---

[3] See Lesson 4, in detail.

[4] It is interesting to note how those ideas were developed, especially because the English parliamentary system – based on the idea of representation – was not rooted in any concept of avant-garde, but on very pragmatic traditions. The difference should be exposed by the fact that the French Revolution was ideologically prepared by secret societies.

Once again, however, England was the only exception to that development because it never introduced the idea of the state as an entity. Instead it preserved the appearance of the old, feudal times, when a variety of organs – the majority of them with a legal personality of their own – were together the equivalent of the unified state. The substance did not vary but, concurrently, the prerogative of the Crown was never abandoned as a concept and it was this feature – the Crown – which could not be accommodated in the role assigned to monarchs in continental Europe.[5]

If the sovereignty belonged to the nation, this did not mean that everybody would have equal rights in its exercise.

The women would be the first to be excepted because they had *infirmitas sexus*; they depended on their fathers and husbands, whose opinions they followed. Therefore there was no reason to give them the right to vote: the right to vote is conditioned by the capacity to form a free and independent judgement on how to vote, which capacity women were not meant to have.

The same reasoning was also valid for the men. Not every man had that freedom of judgement, and in that sense, not everybody was truly equal. Only those who were paying taxes of a certain level would be called upon to exercise the right to vote in the elections. This way the electorate, as proposed by the French Revolution, would be composed of the *bourgeoisie*. Eventually, they made an exception for those who had received a certain level of education, but again, in most cases, the educated people belonged to the *bourgeoisie* anyway. This is the reason why this kind of state was in the hands of one class and thus earned itself the name of the *bourgeois* state.

This state, in the hands of the *bourgeoisie* and based on its twin foundations – the electorate and public administration – perfectly expressed the ideology of the class which was controlling the Parliament and, through this, public administration. It was called the liberal or abstentionist state, because it was meant to leave freedom and space for private initiative. From that point of view, the liberal state's organizational model is also the result of the dominant model for the economy during the same period, as described by Adam Smith's 'invisible hand' and the 'laissez-faire' doctrine. The principle of such free private initiative was not always – and, at times, never – publicly announced in the constitutions, but it was widely considered the basis of the modern state. It meant a positive guarantee of the freedom to exercise free initiative and removed all obstacles to it. Without this, the

---

[5] The prerogative of the Crown is in fact the cradle of all powers which were developed gradually by the states, at least until the concept of national sovereignty was proposed. In the states created or developed in continental Europe in the tradition inaugurated with the French Revolution, there would be no room for discussion about any prerogative of the Crown, because a written, rigid, Constitution was recognized as the only source of state powers. In England, the absence of a written constitution allowed the survival of the prerogative of the Crown, for whatever it might truly mean in our times. It is also true – as explained in various parts of this work – that fragments or remembrances of the prerogative still survive here or there in the constitutional framework of various continental European states.

abstention of the state from any legislative or administrative measure could put obstacles in the way of private initiative.[6]

In reality, the wealth produced under this ideology of the liberal state was again conditioned by state action (and, conversely, inaction). If the French Revolution was the result of the ascension of the *bourgeoisie*, at the end of the day, that *bourgeoisie* would base its new wealth on the exploitation of state property.[7]

The state liquidated its very substantial landed property, which was accumulated over the years as the non-private property of the Crown, because – they said – the state should not be seen as a feudal landlord. The economic activities which were developed so extensively by the absolutist state in all sorts of domains were either closed or sold, especially in the area of defence. The armies had developed all sorts of companies producing everything from bread and armaments to providing catering, and the state left all these activities to the private sector, except where the generals successfully bid to continue provision. Moreover, they considered any assistance or incentive to private initiative as unconstitutional.[8]

Parliament had to control the action of public administration, among other competencies. It was thought that this way, public administration was indirectly lent democratic legitimacy from the sovereign people. Public administration was led by the head of state and – in practice – by the government, collectively by the council of ministers and – individually – ministry by ministry.

The principle of the separation of powers as professed in Europe, considered the administration as 'executive' power of the laws voted upon by Parliament; in theory at least, the executive power was denied any rulemaking authority. Discretionary powers were to be avoided, and the public administration should only execute the will of the sovereign nation.[9] In most cases, the review of the conformity of the Acts of Parliament with the Constitution was left to the Parliaments themselves. Throughout the nineteenth century and at the beginning of the twentieth century, there were many studies and much political action which tried to confine the public administration to an executive role. The result was

---

[6] See the excellent pages of Giannini on those issues, in *Il pubblico potere*, above n 2. A typical example of judicial thinking that mirrors the abstentionist state theory can be found in judgment *Lochner v New York*, 198 US 45 (1905) by the US Supreme Court, whereby it was held that legislation that prohibited bakers from working more than 10 hours a day and 60 hours a week was held unconstitutional as it violated contractual freedom.

[7] This is a part of the history of the state, as proposed by the French Revolution, which was observed by Giannini, because he was able to bring the social sciences into law without, however, losing the legal approach of the institutions. This truth reminds us, in more general terms, that the state is ultimately the most important promoter of the economy, whether the predominant ideology wants an abstentionist state, as well as when it wants an active role of the state in the economy. It could be rightfully observed that, as soon as a political ideology about the role of the state in the economy exhausts its limits in aiding development and prosperity, it is replaced by a new one, quite often in the antipodes of the pre-existing one, which proposes remedies to the failures of the past and a new economic strategy. All hypotheses, however, start from the state, its role, powers and financial capacities.

[8] Giannini, *Il pubblico potere*, above n 2.

[9] This deserves to be stressed, because it precisely reflects what AV Dicey was professing so fervently in England in these times, which, of course, was not a peculiarity of England or of English law, but characteristically political ideology promoted by the liberals all over Europe.

that, up until the Second World War, there was extensive rulemaking by the executive under various names and, correspondingly, little constitutional observance. The development of administrative law as one controlling administrative action only started after the events of 1870–71 in its motherland, France.

The international community started developing administrative law as late as the end of the First World War and – more actively – by the end of the Second World War. Up to that time, the states were omnipotent actors in the international arena and were only restricted by an embryonic customary international law as well as by the international treaties they had signed (at times when they had respected them). In any case, there was no organized international community at that time.

The one-class state did not need political parties, because it was ideologically and politically more or less compact, and the parties were rather groups or clubs either with no true internal rules and principles, or nothing more than mechanisms for electoral purposes. The freedom of association was a long time under question,[10] as it was considered to be falsifying individual freedom; the parties in any contract should be free of any superior influence which could jeopardize the freedom of private initiative.[11]

Successful revolutions, however, always need a mobilization of the masses. Moreover, democratic ideology, combined with freedom of expression, which was guaranteed for all, in combination with gradually-increasing prosperity of the people, plus wars whose outcomes were promising societies a better world, and – most crucial of all – the very features of the new economy and its needs, led, in time, to the multi-class state.

With time the right to vote was extended to more and more social strata. In some states, such as the United States of America first or Greece later on, the voting rights of women were finally accepted everywhere, in some cases, as late as after the Second World War. Every time the boundaries of the electorate were extended, this prepared the way for the next extension. In the meantime, economists of a liberal ideology were always ready to give explanations for new realities and for the ways the states dealt with the economy.[12] State abstention was, however, no longer fashionable by the end of the nineteenth century. On the contrary, public intervention gradually began to dominate to cure 'market failures' and to promote the general interest as identified in the various, burgeoning forms of public utilities and social welfare.[13]

[10] The French Revolution having been hostile to it.

[11] In that sense, N Poulantzas wrote excellent commentry, in *Pouvoir politique et classes sociales* (Paris, Maspero, 1972).

[12] Once more, Giannini, capably discusses the way economists have always been ready to help explain the exceptions gradually introduced to the principles which, in their turn, were bringing change, in *Il pubblico potere*, above n 2.

[13] The common denominator shared by these approaches is the notion of public or general interest which is formed in the jurisprudence. For example, the US Supreme Court, in the case of *Munn v Illinois*, 94 US 113 (1976), held that the storage of grain constituted business vested with a public interest in an attempt to justify public regulation on tariffs. At the same time, across the Atlantic, the Tribunal des Conflits in France, in its *Blanco* judgment of 1873 (see Lesson 2), set the very basis for an

The new technologies – electricity, gas, telegraphs, telephones, railways and so on – were gradually taken over by the states[14] and led to the development of extensive infrastructures. These, in turn, were conditioning a new conception of the role of the state as active supervisor of specific areas of the economy and even direct provider of 'social sensitive' goods and services. Moreover, the states, after having adopted the new technologies, invited private organizations to take over those activities. This was achieved through concessions and thus once again encouraged the production of wealth by the private economy. It was intended that those activities should be adopted by the state as public goals, but that it should be left – as far as possible – to the private economy to execute them,[15] because the state was not meant to do the work of the private economy.[16] Regardless of whether the final provider was a private concessioner or a public undertaking,[17] the institutional design remained the same: such activities were more or less shielded from the rules and challenges of the free market.[18]

This reasoning led the states to continue in the old traditions of the absolutist states, creating works of art in the cities, libraries and public galleries, and so forth, and taking sole responsibility for this.

autonomous administrative law, on the concept of *service d'intérêt général* (in the general interest) that would be followed by the concept of public service.

[14] Or by private entrepreneurs (USA).

[15] In France, the concept of *services publics industriels et commerciaux* (public service, both industrial and commercial) reflects the coexistence of public interest and private economy, since these services are regulated by both public and private law: see Tribunal des Conflits, 22 January 1921, *Société commerciale de l'Ouest Africain* (Bac-d'Eloca). See also B Du Marais, *Droit public de la régulation économique* (Paris, Presses de Sciences Po et Dalloz, 2004).

[16] S Flogaitis, *Les contrats administratifs* (London, Esperia, 1998). The same policies are developing in current times under the name 'public–private partnership' which, as a module, goes beyond the classical concessions. The most important characteristic of the new policies is that they share a comprehensive approach (both at national and international level), towards partnership, with new methods introduced by the advanced financial products proposed by modern economies. The public–private partnership is one more proof that the state and public powers are indeed the main promoter of the production of wealth and prosperity. It is to be noted that in many practices those contracts need – for one reason or another – to go to Parliament for ratification by a formal Act of Parliament. Wherever this is common practice, it must be interpreted on the basis of the historical '*jus politiae*' of the Prince and his right and duty to regulate society; at the same time, all eventual procedural or other illegalities of the contract are resolved by the law. See, for more on this point, S Flogaitis, *Les contrats administratifs*, ibid.

[17] In the USA, apart from post services, other utilities (railways, telecommunications) were provided by private entrepreneurs. By contrast, in France, many of those activities, if not conceded to concessioners, were granted to public monopolies in the form of '*enterprises publiques*'.

[18] The origins of this approach in UK law can be found in a 1787 study by Hale, titled *De Portibus Maris*, in which the author holds that the optimum way to organize sea ports is by establishing a public monopoly. On the other hand in France, a deviation from the free market rules can be established by the fact that a certain activity is closely linked to the public interest and the need to provide a certain service to the public under any circumstances. This theory is illustrated in the three principles of Rolland (Lois de Rolland) on the status of *services publics* (L Rolland, *Précis de droit administratif*, 8th edn (Paris, Dalloz, 1947)). In the USA, the state's choice to organize public utilities such as electricity (*Idaho Power and Light Co v Blomquist* 26 Idaho 222, 141 P 1083 (1914)) and broadcasting (*Carroll Broadcasting Co v FCC* 103 US App DC 346, 258 F.2d 440 (1958)) as a monopoly, was based on the natural monopolies economic theory: the origins of this theory can be traced in JS Mill, *Principles of Political Economy with Some of their Applications to Social Philosophy* (London, Longman, Green and co, 1848). See also, K Train, *Optimal Regulation: The Economic Theory of Natural Monopoly* (Cambridge MA, MIT Press, 1991).

The developing social movements of the time required the states to intervene in the wider area of social management, including the regulation of health, protection of citizens against crime and, most important of all, public education. It is true that the intervention of the state in those areas of the *jus politiae* – and especially in the educational sector – was also needed by the one-class state, because a strong economy needs a healthy, well-protected and educated society. Nonetheless, the better the people were educated, the greater the pressure for political solutions.

The public lawyers proposed a model for what was happening, and they said that the state is a complex organization composed of public services, that is to say, goals which the state adopts as its own, and organizes into services with workers and means, in order to serve the public good. This was the French concept of state from the point of view of the administrative law around the time of the First World War. It was considered a democratic concept, as opposed to the German idea that the state exists because it exercises power, the *Herrschaft*. After the end of the First World War, Duguit could write in his book, *Traité de droit constitutionnel*, that the concept of public service defeated the concept of *Herrschaft* on the battlefields of Verdun.[19]

The same battlefields radically changed the economic environment and the inherent role of the state over the economy. The states went to war and boosted their economies. Such overheating along with a short-lived peace treaty led to a world-scale crisis immediately after the Great War. At that point, constitutionalists and economists[20] agreed that in order to overcome such a crisis, the state would have to adopt an intensified interventionist role and activate itself in many sectors previously left to the markets. The period after the First World War is unique in history, in that the state, irrespective of its political origins (liberal democracy, fascism and communism) became by far the dominant player in any economic field, in view to protect the more vulnerable fragments of society.[21]

---

[19] L Duguit, *Traité de droit constitutionnel*, 3rd edn (Paris, E de Boccard, 1927). This dialogue between Léon Duguit, representative of the so-called 'school of public service' or 'school of Bordeaux', and Maurice Hauriou, representative of the so-called 'school of *Herrschaft*' or 'school of Toulouse', is an excellent example of how scientific positions may easily become caricaturist. Lying behind the two positions is a political philosophy for each one of them, a 'democratic' – distinctly French one – for the former and a more 'autocratic' – distinctly German one – for the latter. Nonetheless, it is not true that Hauriou or his epigones were less democratic than Duguit and his school.

[20] A common point of reference can be found in the theory of John Maynard Keynes on the need for state intervention in the economy; this theory would later serve as the basis for overcoming the effects of the Great Depression in 1929, by enacting the New Deal Policy envisaged by President Roosevelt. See Keynes, 'The End of Laissez-Faire' in *The Collected Writings of John Maynard Keynes*, vol 9 (London, Macmillan, 1972).

[21] Supreme Courts played a vital role to this. In France the Conseil d'Etat increased the number of economic activities falling under the concept of *services publics*: the distribution of drinkable water (CE 6.5.1931, *Tondut*) and transportation (CE 29.1.1932, *Compagnie des autobus antibois*), was followed by the extinguishing of hazardous reptiles! (CE 6.2.1903, *Terrier*). In the USA, it would be judicially held that certain businesses were 'vested with a public interest', and subject to public regulation. Examples include the distribution of ice (*New State Ice Co v Liebmann*, 285 US 262 (1932)) and the retail of milk (*Nebbia v New York*, 291 US 502 (1934)).

All these radical social and economic changes gradually made the one-class state evolve into something far more complex.

Towards the Multi-class State

The trade unions and other working class organizations did not need the right to vote in general elections in order to develop – either legally or illegally. They only needed freedom of association, freedom of expression and freedom of the press, among others. The political parties followed suit, especially when the lower socio-economic strata gained the right to vote.[22]

At the beginning, the parties were largely representative of a single class within society. In the first place, the political parties of the working class or of those working in agriculture felt the need to resist the system and advance a new concept for the organization of society. But other parts of that society also had a need to create organizations with which to defend their interests. In the meantime, the associations of industrialists and of commerce – among others – started developing their own activities and defending their interests. It was the same with their political organization, which was now needed in order to oppose the organized requests of the lower socio-economic strata of society, and so the times witnessed the rise of parties representing them.

In contrast with previous groupings, the political parties were a permanent organization of political forces. They took this organized shape in order to mobilize the society, collect votes and be properly represented in the elections. They had a political programme – in other words, an ideology and a strategy – which could eventually bring them to power, execute the proposed political programme and make the state serve their own vision of society. Therefore, they became one of the public powers and, in this way, they developed in the various countries according to the political and legal traditions of each one of them. In some countries they were covered by general legislation for the associations, in others, by special legislation for the political parties, and so on. They often produced a developed system of internal life with all sorts of rules, and became bureaucratic

---

[22] The most characteristic example is the changes which were brought into British political life by the Reform Act of 1867, which changed the composition of Parliament which, up to then, had represented the middle classes. Representation in Parliament was enlarged by the introduction of household suffrage, which initially brought into the electorate the artisans of the cities and, secondly, the best paid members of the working class. WI Jennings wrote on these issues in *The Law and the Constitution,* 2nd edn (London, University of London Press, 1959) 315. SA de Smith observed the following a propos of the same reform: 'With the enfranchisement of the urban artisan class, Parliament discovered a new concern for public education, public health and other rudimentary social services, and trade unionism received the full accolade of legitimacy. The age of collectivism began to flourish. The passage of the second Reform Act, moreover, gave impetus to a new development, of the greatest constitutional importance – the organization of mass political parties on a national scale', in *Constitutional and Administrative Law,* 6th edn (London, Penguin, 1990) 241. Also, see S Flogaitis, *Administrative Law et droit administratif* (Paris, LDGJ, 1986) at 64.

organizations, working in parallel with – and sometimes of equal importance to – the state administrations.[23]

The political parties representing the workers and lower socio-economic strata of society – brimming, as they were, with various socialist ideas – put forward a totally different agenda to the one of the abstentious, liberal state. In contrast, they asked for interventionism, they wanted a state which would intervene in, and protect the workers from, capitalism, and which would provide assistance to the poor, good health protection, education for all and professional training. Some of them asked for the passage of entire sectors of the economy to come under direct state control, especially where the activities were monopolistic in character. This was sometimes extended even further, with the desire to see the entire economy becoming public property.[24]

In a country with general voting rights it is not possible to govern without compromises[25] and gradually many of these ideas were adopted. This was because parts of the older society found them more humane whilst others wanted to avoid potentially worse options. Eventually, influenced by the process of that political struggle, a new, homogenized society would emerge in every country.

The Multi-class State

At the turn of the twentieth century – and particularly after the First World War – with the extension of the right to vote to all male citizens and the introduction (in certain countries) of an electoral system of proportional representation, the state had finally become – for once and for all – a multi-class state.

The most important and striking feature of this new era was the development of a new class, the so-called middle class, composed mainly of working people who, nevertheless, did not see themselves as part of the traditional working class and which had determined interests, identity and ideology of its own. Politically, this middle class rarely aligned itself with political forces promoting forms of state outside the tradition of the liberal state. In addition, all political parties needed its support – either fully or partially – in order to obtain the sheer numbers of votes which would allow them to have power.[26]

---

[23] See the classics: M Ostrogorski, *Democracy and the Organizations of Political Parties* (London, Macmillan, 1902); R Michels, *Political Parties, a Sociological Study of the Oligarchical Tendencies of Modern Democracy* (New York, Hearst's International Library Co, 1915); M Duverger, *Les partis politiques* (Rais, Armand Colin, 1951).

[24] A Svolos, *Le Travail dans le Constitutions contemporaines* (Paris, Librairie du Receuil Sirey, 1939), with a Preface by J Barthélemy and B Mirkine-Guetzévitch.

[25] See H Kelsen, 'On the Essence and Value of Democracy' (1929) in A Jacobson and B Schlink (eds), *Weimar, A Jurisprudence of Crisis* (Oakland, University of California Press, 2000) 84.

[26] Giannini makes this observation which, again, comes from the social sciences, in *Il pubblico potere*, above n 2.

In the multi-class state, the ideology of those exercising public power and, therefore, the ideology of the state is neither given, nor permanent, but depends on the political programme of those who have been elected in the last elections, and on the duration of their power. This is the reason why the constitutions acquired an importance which they had never had before. From the position of documents providing for the distribution of power within the tripartite division of the state functions, they became complex legal documents, synthesizing a variety of ideologies and political dreams of the various components of the nation at that given time.[27]

For the first time, therefore, the electoral system became a very important issue. The electoral system which was – in one sense or another – a variation of the uninominal constituency, served well in the times of the one-class state. However, it was not long before it was not seen as such by the many ascending political forces around Europe at this time, when the electoral body and the nation were finally concurring. Proportional representation[28] was the electoral system promoted by many in times where the general elections were no longer a pure procedure, but an emergent, unique form of political struggle.[29]

Apart from what was included in the Constitution, the newly-evolved multi-class state was ideologically neutral. In its infancy, this kind of state lacked experience, and the anxieties of the dominant strata of society about a future which could not be controlled as it had been before, in tandem with the forceful push of the lower classes towards power, introduced a new, world-wide uncertainty as to how modern states should be organized. In post-First World War times, when people were looking for a fresh start, the system of 'one man – one vote' was not yet well-rooted in the political systems. Alongside this, new ideas about the way societies should be organized were advancing, especially those of corporatism and communism.

In countries exhibiting weak structures, this led to other forms of state; particularly notable cases were fascism in Italy (and even Spain, Portugal and Greece for

[27] Especially because several public policies are now covered by, or reflected in, the constitutions, and are therefore not subject to easy change or to any change at all. See also, among others, D Grimm, *Die Zukunft der Verfassung* (Frankfurt am Main, Suhrkamp, 1991).

[28] The author who studied and presented to the wider legal community the notion of proportional representation, and who was acknowledged for this by L Duguit, in the text itself of his book on constitutional law, was N Saripolos, *La démocratie et l'élection proportionnelle, Etude historique, juridique et politique* (Paris, A Rousseau, 1899).

[29] Mainly because in the system of majority vote in uninominal constituencies, the remaining votes of the parties which do not produce the winner of the seat are lost, in terms of national vote, and therefore it is possible that a party may obtain the majority of the seats without gaining the majority of the votes nationwide. Weaker social groups could thus never be represented in Parliament outside systems of proportional representation. In England, where there is a historic tradition for majority vote and uninominal constituencies, the system survived because of the concurrence of the two main political forces – Conservatives and Labour – in the drafting of the constituencies (especially as safe or unsafe constituencies of one or the other) thus absorbing the negative effects of the remaining unused votes. Nonetheless, the system can become questionable, when the majority in Parliament advances reform not supported in the constituencies where, in any case, it had no support. This is because it will continue losing them with greater disparity when compared with the other party, without any influence on the total number of seats countrywide.

a period of time), and Nazism in Germany. In the East, the Bolsheviks took power in the Russian Empire and created the Soviet Union.

The Fascist State[30]

The Bolshevik Revolution of 1917 and the end of the First World War constituted very difficult times for the states of Europe. Not only was a new kind of political organization of societies successful in a country as important as Russia, but also Western Europe was exhausted by a war which had so obviously been conducted because every European power was trying to enlarge its own market and economy. As the armies had been based on conscription, social unease, especially in the lower strata of the society, combined with the fear of the social strata which had produced the one-class state of the nineteenth century. Many feared that the possible outcomes of the situation could create a very unstable future for many countries. Those were the times when the multi-class state was in its infancy, and the states had not yet developed the institutions, procedures and practices to absorb the impact of social evolution, or they were not yet used to them.

This situation provoked fascism in countries with weaker politico–financial systems.[31] Italy, Spain, Portugal (Germany experienced this in the form of Nazism) but Greece also did the same for a short period of time, and many other countries around the globe introduced a new political experience. It should be remembered that this experience evolved over 20 years before it collapsed in Italy with the war, and similarly evolved over more than 40 years in Spain or Portugal. These were not short episodes in the life of states, but very specific answers to the need for political organization of societies.

Paradoxically, fascism is not a system which negates the multi-class state. It is a political system that believes that it can bring all within society into state institutions and allow the society to operate through the state.[32] At the same time it is a

---

[30] The fascist state as opposed to the Nazi state; fascism was a certain way of organizing public powers; it spread far and wide in the world and was not a peculiarity of a certain society. Nazism was a brutal German regime, sharing many characteristics of fascism, but not reflecting it in its entirety. However, its ideology and the institutions which it proposed have been widely and thoroughly examined, so Nazism will not be part of this study. See, among others, F Neumann Behemoth, *The Structure and Practice of National Socialism, 1033–1944* (Oxford, Oxford University Press, 1972); J Caplan, *Government without Administration, State and Civil Service in Weimar and Nazi Germany* (Oxford, Clarendon Press, 1988); P Madden, *Adolf Hitler and the Nazi Epoch, an Annotated Bibliography of English-language Works on the Origins, Nature and Structure of the Nazi State* (Lanham MD, Scarecrow Press; Pasadena CA, Salem Press, 1998); PD Stachura, *The Shaping of the Nazi State* (London, Croom Helm, 1978); GC Browder, *Foundations of the Nazi Police State, the Formation of Sipo and SD* (Lexington, University Press of Kentucky, 1990).

[31] An excellent study on fascism and dictatorship was written by N Poulantzas, *Fascisme et Dictature*, 2nd edn (Paris, Seuil/Maspero, 1974).

[32] S Cassese wrote an excellent book on the fascist state, *Lo stato fascista* (Bologna, Il Mulino, 2010), where there is also further bibliography. See also, H Heller, *Europa und der Fascismus* (Berlin-Leipzig, Walter de Gruyter, 1929); HW Schneider, *Making the Fascist State* (Oxford, Oxford University Press,

political system based on autocratic principles through the way in which it is organized, and whether or not it constituted totalitarianism is a question still debated by political scientists.

Looking through that particular lens, fascism did not abolish either the institutions or the legislation of the state as it was before. It kept the existing system and simultaneously created new institutions parallel to the existing ones. The existing ones gradually lost their power in real terms, while the new ones exercised power in the way fascism understood it.

In other words, fascism was a system of organizing the state, which provided very specific answers to the challenges facing the multi-class state during its infancy, and in some countries the ruling classes were afraid of facing these.

In short, fascists believed that all the antagonisms of the multi-class society could be brought under the umbrella of the state and be successfully represented by it.

Rocco, Minister of Justice, reporting on the Law for the Secret Societies, stated:

> The national State, that is the fascist State, has undertaken a struggle against all the forces of disorganization which were developed in the core of the State and gradually destroying its sovereignty. The State must dominate . . . all the forces existing in the country, and cannot accept, as it was unfortunately accepted for a long time, the existence of powerful organizations, such as the Confederation of the labour, the Associations of those working in the railways, the post, the telegraph, the sailors or the tramway people, or, finally such as the Masonry, which are the effective patrons of the nation's life.[33]

Six years earlier, in 1932, Mussolini, had attempted to distil the essence of fascism in the *Italian Encyclopaedia*:

> For the fascist, everything is in the state, nothing human or spiritual exists, and even less has any value, outside the State. . . Neither individuals, nor groups (political parties, associations, trade unions, social classes) outside the State. The one which can bring solutions to the dramatic contradictions of capitalism is the State.[34]

In order to achieve that goal, fascism introduced corporatism into public institutions and reinterpreted an old idea in its own way.[35]

Corporatism has its roots in various areas of the development of modern societies, but in terms of organized theory, it seems that it was other European societies' version of the egalitarianism of the French Revolution. In Austria, Adam

---

1928); D Thompson, *State Control in Fascist Italy, Culture and Conformity, 1925–43* (Manchester, Manchester University Press, 1991).

[33] A Rocco, *Legge sulle società segrete, Scritti e discorsi politici di Alfredo Rocco, III, La formazione dello Stato fascista (1925–34)* (Milano, Giuffrè, 1938) 797 and 802, cited by Cassese, in *Lo Stato fascista,* ibid.

[34] B Mussolini, 'Fasismo' in *Enciclopedia Italiana,* vol XIV (Roma, Istituto della Enciclopedia Italiana, 1932) 848 and 850, cited by Cassese, *Lo Stato fascista,* ibid; also published in English as, *Fascism, Doctrine and Institutions* (New York, H Fertig, 1968).

[35] HD Goad, *The Making of the Corporate State, a Study of Fascist Development* (London, Christophers, 1934); for special attention to Germany, see D Sweeney, *Work, Race and the Emergence of Radical Right Corporatism in Imperial Germany* (Ann Arbor, University of Michigan Press, 2009).

Müller[36] proposed the class-state which mirrored those of the Central and Eastern European countries. This stood opposed to the French doctrines and was based on the organization of classes in corporations. The idea of organizing the society through corporations rather than through egalitarianism was also promoted by some socialist movements or Christian syndicalism; renowned public lawyers – such as Léon Duguit[37] – were promoting the idea that public entities producing goods for society should be governed by a *syndicalism fonctionariste*.

Fascism used corporatism as the way to bring every human activity into the state. Every human activity must be organized into a state institution, no matter whether or not they were antagonistic to each other. All interests should be served through the state and no human activity could be tolerated outside the state. In this way the society was totally controlled by the state and by those who had the power.

The third challenge that fascism faced was the difficulties experienced at that time in history, of finding equilibrium between the doctrinal position that the executive should not legislate and the real needs faced by any democratic state for the speedy production of rules. Fascism's answer was autocracy at the head of the fascist movement, and to devolve all rulemaking powers to that autocrat.

Rulemaking parliaments and various councils existed, especially because fascism did not abolish the organs of the pre-existing state but rather created several other parallel ones mainly belonging to the party,[38] or else inspired by corporatism. Their rulemaking power, however, was merely nominal.[39]

Fascism collapsed for many reasons which have been studied in detail by authors of all specializations. It was – in its own very original way – an attempt to bring states back to the times of the absolutist state whilst possessing the appearance of a multi-class state.

Corporatism survived the fascist state, particularly because this idea was not produced, but was only used, by it. In several countries and constitutions of the post-Second World War period, institutions inspired by the idea of corporatism were created and introduced.[40]

---

[36] In Giannini, *Il pubblico potere*, above n 2.

[37] L Duguit, *Traité de droit constitutionnel*, 3rd edn, vols II and III, *La théorie générale de l'État* (Paris, Ed de Boccard, 1928–30); also, *Etudes de droit public*, vol II, *L'Etat, les gouvernants et les agents* (Paris, A Fontemoing, 1903); S Flogaitis, *La notion de décentralisation en France, en Allemagne et en Italie* (Paris, LGDJ, 1979) 45.

[38] *Partito Nazionale Fascista, Il Gran Consiglio nei primi cinque anni dell'era fascista* (Roma, Libreria del Littorio, 1927); P Cavallaro, *Il Gran Consiglio del fascismo, Organo anfibio tra partito e stato*, (Siracusa, Lombardi, 2004); R Lazzero, *Partito Nazionale Fascista* (Milano, Rizzoli, 1985).

[39] For a detailed survey of the institutions brought by fascism, see Cassese, *Lo stato fascista*, above n 32.

[40] Among others, see S Berger and H Compston (eds), *Policy Concertation and Social Partnership in Western Europe, Lessons from the Twenty-First Century* (New York, Berghahn Books, 2002); P Pasture, G Devos and CA Davids (eds), *Changing Liaisons, the Dynamics of Social Partnership in Twentieth Century West-European Democracies* (Brussels, Peter Lang, 2007); O Newman, *The Challenge of Corporatism* (London, Macmillan, 1981); S Vickerstaff and J Sheldrake, *The Limits of Corporatism, the British Experience in the Twentieth Century* (Aldershot, Avebury Press, 1989); JE Reade, *Town Planning and the 'Corporatism Thesis'* (Wolverhampton, 1980).

The State of the Bolshevik[41] Revolution[42]

Aside from its ideology and political programme, the Bolshevik Revolution had various features, some of them going back to the French Revolution and its mechanisms, others to do with the peculiarities of Russia at the beginning of the twentieth century. Until the October Revolution, the only experiment of socialist governance was the famous Commune de Paris, so much exalted in the collective dreams of the socialist movements at that time.

The Bolshevik Revolution was meant to be the revolution of all the people – especially of the oppressed working classes – however guided by the Communist Party which represented their interests. The party had the ability to conceive future policies and produce the means to make them effective; it was therefore, by definition, the avant-garde of the society, and considered that it deserved to steer developments in the society and the state.[43]

It is the same way of thinking as that of the French Revolution, the difference relies on the fact that the French Revolution was prepared by a societal avant-garde, which, however, did not have to be organized in a party or an organized force. This was mainly because the state produced was a one-class state and the Constitution of 1791 guaranteed the representative character of the political system. In both systems, the revolution was prepared by the elite, was executed by the people and would be exercised by the elite which prepared it. Most significantly, more than a century had passed between the two events and European societies had produced political parties, a novelty in comparison with the French Revolution.

The party would represent the interest of the people, because the party had the knowledge to do so; it was the bearer of the new science of scientific materialism – or Marxism – and had the intellectual power to promote and propel society in an organized way.[44]

---

[41] H Kelsen, *The Political Theory of Bolshevism, a Critical Analysis* (Berkeley, University of California Press, 1948); G Poggi, *The State, its Nature, Development and Prospects* (Stanford, Stanford University Press, 1991), and in Italian, *Lo Stato: natura, sviluppo, prospettive* (Bologna, Il Mulino, 1992) 219.

[42] The remarks made here do not intend, of course, to exhaust a discussion which – during the existence of the USSR – was very intense, and out of which nothing was left after the collapse of the regime. They only intend to discuss the peculiarities of the state proposed by the Bolsheviks in the general frame of this book.

[43] A Levine, *The General Will, Rousseau, Marx, Communism* (Cambridge, Cambridge University Press, 1993).

[44] Among others, see JF Triska (ed), *Communist Party-states, Comparative and International Studies* (Indianapolis, Bobbs-Merrill, 1969); R Miliband, *Marxism and Politics* (Oxford, Oxford University Press, 1977); D Tarschys, *Beyond the State, the Future Polity in Classical and Soviet Marxism* (Stockholm, Laromedelsforlaget, 1972); J Ehrenberg, *The Dictatorship of the Proletariat, Marxism's Theory of Socialist Democracy* (New York, Routledge, 1992); M Neocleous, *The Fabrication of Social Order, a Critical Theory of Political Power* (London, Pluto Press, 2000); AZ Kaminski, *An Institutional Theory of Communism Regimes, Design, Function and Breakdown* (San Francisco, ICS Press, 1992).

The other characteristic of the times was that the Bolsheviks reversed an absolutist state, which was well-rooted in the hearts of the Russian people through centuries. Russia had not gone through any form of democratic process either of the multi-class state – which was the rule in societies of those times – or even that of the one-class state.

The Bolsheviks did not want to destroy that powerful state of absolutism. It was useful to the Revolution and its purpose of changing the world – at least within the boundaries of the newly-established Soviet Union – because it was powerful. They replaced the Tsar with the Communist Party, which was called upon to govern the country in the name of the dictatorship of the proletariat.

The main ideas forming the basis for the new state were the abolition of private property and the development of a plan for the economy and society.

As for the system of government, its purpose was exalting the role of the state. Nothing could be done outside the state; everything was done within it.[45] The state was run by the party, and although deliberative organs of all sorts were deployed throughout both country and hierarchy of the state, it was the upper organs of the state, that is to say, of the party controlling the state, which were responsible for all decisions and for guiding the people. This system was called democratic centralism.[46]

Thus, the state created by the Bolshevik Revolution was another answer to the multi-class state with its potential to develop societies. The multi-class state was meant to be the warrantor of the evolution of institutions and the society. The state promoted by the Bolshevik Revolution gave the state the role of changing society in the name of public interest as expressed by the Communist Party, which was – in effect – the sole expression of the interests of the dominant class, the proletariat.

As the ideology of the conquered state was absolutist and the Communist Party established the dictatorship of the proletariat, the interpretation of the idea of the public interest by the state – as a reason of deviation from the rule of law – became too easy.

Government by-planning survived the Soviet State, however, and it became an idea which hugely influenced the European democracies of the post-Second World War period. Planning institutions for the economy with a view to guaranteeing development, as well as urban or territorial planning, were both ideas which were adopted almost everywhere in Western Europe, especially in the 1950s and 1960s.

---

[45] From this point of view the Bolshevik state shares the same approach as fascism, something which animated endless discussions around the world in the times of the USSR. History proved that only the multi-class state could promote pluralism and polycentrism of public powers.

[46] See the analysis by TH Rigby, 'A Conceptual Approach to Authority, Power and Police in Soviet Union' in TH Rigby, A Brown and P Reddaway (eds), *Authority, Power and Policy in the USSR. Essays Dedicated to Leonard Shapiro* (London, Macmillan, 1980).

The Second World War and the Multi-class State

The multi-class state triumphed after the Second World War. It was based on the constitutions of a new generation which aimed to guarantee personal freedom and dignity, introduce constitutional courts[47] (especially in countries which had witnessed important diversions from such principles in their recent history) and, according to the cases presented to it, provide answers to questions of govern-ance.

Those new constitutions would introduce, in varied but clear terms, the prin-ciple of the equality of all in law which, in electoral terms, would mean one per-son, one vote. This way, all discussion and debate undertaken between the two wars about various systems of representation – such as family vote and corporatist vote – would be excluded from the main political representations of the nations.[48]

Most important of all, however, was the fact that the states would now be called upon to create all sorts of international organizations, and to give up parts of their national sovereignty for a common international good. The Bretton Woods Agreements would take this a step further: they would propose international institutions regulating the economic development of the people and of the states. Thus they became promoters of continuous institutional change worldwide, encouraging more and more integration of states, policies and of practices based on a common way of understanding humanity and the world. With the collapse of the Soviet Union, this process became yet more coherent.

The state in the new era, therefore, displayed features which were entirely new.

The most important of these features was that the potential for division between the legitimacy of the Parliament as representation of the people, and the executive as representation of the authority, no longer existed. Governments were accepted as having the same legitimacy as Parliaments and public adminis-tration as having its own legitimacy which came from the Constitution itself.

---

[47] If the nineteenth century was the century of Parliaments, then the twentieth century was one of constitutional justice. In fact, in the multi-class state, the necessity for compromise among both social and political forces, created the conditions for the introduction of a constitutional justice. It should be remembered here that the scholar who introduced the idea of a constitutional justice was H Kelsen, of the Weimar era. See H Kelsen, 'La garantie juridictionnelle de la Constitution', (1928) 35 *Revue du droit public et de la science politique* 197. For the development of constitutional justice after the Second World War see, among many others: M Fromont, *La justice constitutionnelle dans le monde* (Paris, Dalloz, 1996); L Favoreu, *Les cours constitutionnelles* (Paris, PUF, 1986); D Rousseau, *La justice constitutionnelle en Europe* (Paris, Montchrestien, 1992); and T Groppi, 'Giustizia costituzionale comparata' in S Cassese (a cura di), *Dizionario di diritto pubblico*, III (Milano, Giuffrè, 2006) 2790.

[48] The American influence on the reorganization of European political thought and structures is evident, not only in countries which underwent occupation – such as Germany – but also in every other country which received American aid, especially in the promotion of constitutional courts, human rights, human dignity and democratic institutions based on the idea of one man – one vote. Those principles triumphed, Europe-wide, with the fall of the Berlin wall in 1989.

Correspondingly, many constitutions introduced rules favouring governments and their stability.[49]

The state and the executive are no longer monolithic, not only because it is generally accepted – and is indeed common practice – that many other entities, regardless of public or private law, may exist and act within the state, but also because a series of new organs, independent from state authority, have been created. These are entrusted with the regulation of important areas of public life, and include bodies governing television broadcasting, and antitrust, among many others.

This new way of organizing public power finds its origins in the American concept of public organization, reflected mainly in the Administrative Procedure Act of 1946. This document would – over time – influence concepts, ideas and ways of understanding public administration worldwide. Such influence would be particularly marked in European countries, thanks, inter alia, to the work of specialized international organizations, such as the OECD (Organization for Economic Co-operation and Development) or the World Bank. The notion of independent administrative authorities migrated across the Atlantic, as did public inquiries as a tool of the lawmaking process, as well as transparency issues and others.

Gradually, international political organizations, such as the United Nations, started producing legislation in areas such as combating terrorism, money laundering and human trafficking, to name but a few. This had either direct or indirect effects upon legislation in every country of the world.[50] This burgeoning development in the legal world was assisted by the most recently adopted constitutions, which give a predominant place to the internal hierarchy of legal norms including international law. Generally, these remain superior to the Acts of Parliament, and sometimes even to the Constitution itself.[51]

The state has also witnessed the alteration of the core of the executive, in other words, the Council of Ministers. The ministries no longer monolithically represent the public interest. Instead, quite often each one of them represents interests antagonistic with those served by others. For instance, the Ministry of Agriculture does not always represent converging interests with the Ministry for the Protection of the Environment which, again, often represents the opposite interests of the Ministry of Public Works, and so forth.

In this new political and legal situation, the states and their democratic legitimacy have evolved a long way from the days of their infancy, after the national democratic revolutions and aspirations of the eighteenth and nineteenth centuries. The development of democratic societies took unexpected twists and turns,

---

[49] This is the result of specific policies advanced after the Second World War, because one of the reasons which brought fascism and Nazism to power was political and governmental instability. See also, PH Lavaux, *Parlementarisme rationalisé et stabilité du pouvoir exécutif* (Bruxelles, Bruylant, 1988).

[50] *Internationalization of Public Law – Proceedings of the European Group of Public Law Conference 2005*, European Public Law Series, vol LXXXIII (London, Esperia, 2006).

[51] A first generation of constitutions demonstrating clauses of this kind are those which were drafted especially in view of the European communities; a second generation followed after the fall of the Berlin wall, the latter being even more open to international law.

and the reason for these is that, in state building, there are no universal truths but rather a continuous evolution and adaptation to needs and responses to situations presented.

Last but not least, the state has altered horizontally. It is no longer the one and only source of legitimate public power. This is because of changes such as federalism, regionalization or devolution and any other possible scheme that political life could introduce in the future.

Democratic State, State of Law, Social State[52]

Each of these three concepts find their origins in the social sciences and particularly in political science. Nonetheless, they have acquired legal significance thanks, especially, to the works of German scholars after the Second World War and to the introduction of the Fundamental Law (*Grundgesetz* (GG)).

The concept of democratic state traditionally means everything and nothing, particularly because this is a title which the state has repeatedly lent itself since the French Revolution, both during the times of the one-class state and even more so since the introduction of the multi-class state. The same concept was also used by the Communist states, and it is important to stress that they wanted to monopolize it for themselves, the traditional states being considered as class states and therefore not democratic.

The concept acquired significance in public law as *democratic principle*,[53] an idea proposed by German post-War authors. Democratic principle is understood as a series of rules and principles transcending the democracies established in our times by the constitutions, and together composing an ethical and legal canvas of attitudes which society and state need to promote in democracies. These include transparency, accountability, openness, majority voting and dignity in exercising public powers. Many other principles have also derived from the democratic

[52] The normative school of Vienna taught that the state and the law are one and the same, see H Kelsen, *Pure Theory of Law* (M Knight tr, Berkeley, University of California Press, 1970); also, *General Theory of Norms* (M Hartney tr, Oxford, Clarendon Press, 1991); also, *General Theory of Law and State* (A Wedberg tr, Cambridge MA, Harvard University Press, 1949); L Vinx, *Hans Kelsen's Pure Theory of Law, Legality and Legitimacy* (Oxford, Oxford University Press, 2007) as its most distinguished representative, although A Merkl, *Allgemeines Verwaltungsrecht* (Wien, Berlin, Springer, 1927) must not be forgotten. The present study did not enter into theories of state which, no matter how much they have influenced legal thought, remain entirely products of mind and not of political evolution. For an excellent account on the state of law, see J Chevallier, *L'Etat de droit* (Paris, Montchrestien, 2003); also, P Costa, 'Lo Stato di diritto, Un'introduzione storica' in P Costa and D Zolo (eds), *Lo stato di diritto: storia, teoria, critica* (Milano, Feltrinelli, 2006); G Gozzi, 'Stato di diritto e diritti soggettivi nella storia costituzionale tedesca' ibid at 260; L Ferrajoli, 'Lo Stato di diritto fra passato e futuro' ibid at 349.

[53] There is extended bibliography on these issues. See, for the leading contributions: E-W Böckenförde, *Gesetz und gesetzgebende Gewalt*, 2nd edn (Berlin, Duncker und Humblot, 1981); *Recht, Staat, Freiheit* (Frankfurt, Shurkamp, 1991); also, 'Demokratie als Verfassungsprinzip' in J Isensee and P Kirchhof, *Handbuch des Staatsrechts der Bundesrepublik Deutschland*, II (Heidelberg, CF Müller, 2003) 429.

principle, all of which increase demands for a more democratic society and state.

In recent times – and especially in the 1970s and the 1980s – new activities have been undertaken by European states with the aim of introducing the democratic principle into public administration. New instruments have been adopted, especially those of a contractual character and forms of concerted action between the state and private initiative, among others.

The concept of the state of law (*Rechtsstaat*) meant that the state must obey the law and – in general terms – it agreed with the rule of law and the principle of legality.[54] In a certain way, it was the prerequisite of the democratic principle. It should also be remembered that both state of law and social state are mentioned in the *Nassauer Denkschrift* of Freiherr vom Stein in 1807, as the goals that his country and society should set for itself.

By social state,[55] I mean the welfare state, which is the state that takes positive action in order to provide services of social character to the people. It does this through the public services which the Constitution or other sources of legality have established. It is a principle which transcends modern constitutions providing for it, in parallel with the democratic principle. In most European societies today, the social state is considered part of the material Constitution and is one of the fundamentals of European civilization.

The Classless State?[56]

The multi-class state has opened up a great deal, and this certainly includes the political participation of all within society, in other words, to all the forces of the nation. Thus it has lost any reason to be so-called because it references an attribute – classlessness – which is important for reminding the *iter* of the development of the concept of state, but which became meaningless as soon as the *iter* was concluded. If Massimo Severo Giannini was still among us, he would perhaps call the result of this *iter* 'classless' state, an institution where the social strata composing the society and represented in the electorate are important from the point of view of the social sciences, but which have no importance anymore – from the point of view of public law – for what concerns the concept of state.

---

[54] It needs to be said that the term 'principle of legality' better expresses what it means than the term 'rule of law'. When Jèze translated Dicey into French, he translated the rule of law as '*règne de la loi*' which, again, is more explicit than the original one.

[55] Giannini considers the social state as a concept of political science rather than as a legal one, in 'Stato sociale, una nozione inutile' in *Scritti in onore di Costantino Mortati* (Milano, Giuffrè, 1977) 141.

[56] After a suggestion of David Feldman.

Lesson 7

The 'Modern' State Integrating in the International Community

In recent years, the modern state has developed in a completely changed environment, as the economy has globalized, and private companies have acquired gigantesque dimensions in comparison with the average state. The international community is developing quickly, at a pace never seen before. In this environment, the state is moving into new roles and yet – beyond that – the concept of state is affected in its core elements.[1]

The globalization of the economy was an inevitable result of capitalism, as Karl Marx and Friedrich Engels had already foreseen in The Communist Manifesto.[2] When capitalism exhausted the possibilities offered by the integrated markets of national states, it had access to the opportunities offered by regional organizations such as the European Union, or markets created by federal or regional states of all kinds with huge dimensions, such as the United States of America, Brazil, Australia, India, China and the Russian Federation. The globalized economy has integrated all resources in a system which is not possible to control, at least in the traditional way, by any state or any group. This introduces a question mark over whether globalization is truly a system, or rather just a way for the world's economy to exist.

---

[1] This simple truth made many – if not most – of the world's constitutional lawyers opposed to globalization, because they cannot adapt the fundamentals of traditional constitutional law to which they are accustomed, into the new situation. As civil liberties are traditionally the result of a dialogue between the individual and the state, echoing the German concept of the dialogue between state and society, constitutional lawyers have difficulties applying the concepts they know to the newly-emerging world. Therefore, they often defend the state, which was traditionally seen as the enemy of civil liberties, and exalt it as the protector of civil liberties. The point, however, is not to be in favour of or against globalization, because it exists whether we like it or not; the challenge is to develop new systems for the protection of the citizens against public powers in a globalized world. There are many important studies about the issues addressed in this chapter, as for example, J Chevalier, L'Etat post-moderne, 2nd edn (Paris, LGDJ, 2004); also S Mannoni, 'Stato nazionale di diritto e diritto internazionale' in P Costa and D Zolo (eds), Lo Stato di diritto: storia, teoria, critica (Milano, Feltrinelli, 2006) 485; G Poggi, Lo Stato. Natura, Sviluppo, Prospettive (Bologna, Il Mulino, 1992) 193 (ch VIII, 'Lo stato liberal-democratico nel secolo ventesimo', II).

[2] K Marx and F Engels, The Communist Manifesto (London, Phoenix, 1996); FL Bender (ed), Karl Marx, The Communist Manifesto, Prefaces by Marx and Engels, annotated text (New York, London, Norton, 1988); JC Isaac (ed), Karl Marx, Friedrich Engels, The Communist Manifesto (New Haven, Yale University Press, 2012); P Gasper (ed), Karl Marx, Friedrich Engels, The Communist Manifesto: A Road Map to History's Most Important Document (Chicago, Haymarket Books, 2005).

In the globalized era, money transfers cannot be stopped by the states. The activities of multinational companies – even the smallest activity – can proceed into forum shopping and become established in the country offering the best conditions. In the same way, it can migrate to any other state at any time and easily, without the first or the second state being able to do anything to stop it. If they did try to stop the economic freedom of any company, that state would immediately risk being severely attacked by the international press and interested groups, with potentially disastrous economic results. The transfer of goods, and – in large measure – of people, does not recognize frontiers and it would be a catastrophe for any advanced economy to try to reintroduce them. The euro zone countries have adopted a common currency by giving up a considerable portion of the state's traditional sovereignty.

Beyond the economy, at the same time, the system of values on which a modern society should be based has been globalized[3] and mechanisms are developing around the globe for making sure that everyone and every state, or holder of public power, abides by that system.

All of this has happened because the states have taken the necessary legal steps to make it happen. In any case, the states had little choice because they could not stop it. The states have always been the main promoters of the economy and they cannot escape from that role.

A Fragmented and Simultaneously Integrated International Environment

There has always been international life and the agreements made by the Roman emperors with the Persians in the seventh century are illustrative of this.[4] International lawyers have established the Treaty of Westphalia as the symbolic starting point of modern international law.[5] The international life of the times – the omnipotence of the 'modern' state – witnessed many important attempts to organize various aspects of international state activity. This was mainly done through treaties proposed and adhered to by states, but also, gradually, by the development of customary international law. This reflected all the shared ethical values and legal principles of humanity and has thus become an identification for a progressing, civilized international community. However, the initial breakthrough in the development of international law was the end of the First World

---

[3] Global media, the social media and, more generally, the internet, are playing this role very effectively: promoting values, behaviours, and American English, especially to the youth of the world.

[4] Following the struggle over the Holy Land. The treaty has always been an international instrument of the regulation of relations between powers.

[5] WP Guthrie, *The Later Thirty Years' War, from the Battle of Wittstock to the Treaty of Westphalia* (London, Greenwood Press, 2003).

War through the introduction of the League of Nations.[6] Although that experiment in no way equalled the United Nations, which followed later, it had the accolade of being the first permanent attempt to organize international life. The failure of the League of Nations contributed to more international integration in the longer term, albeit through a Second World War. Once again, this involved treaties and agreements which were discussed and signed, this time on American soil.

The United Nations, which was permanently established on American soil, would create a functional forum and an instrument for peace and progress in the world. Meanwhile the Bretton Woods international organizations became instruments for development and continuous institutional change around the globe within both the states and in the international community. For the first time the historically omnipotent states were abdicating important parts of their sovereignty and declaring themselves ready to contribute to the development of a new, increasingly integrated, international arena. The atrocities and organized crime of the Nazis, and several other recent regimes, helped to introduce the idea of a baseline of human dignity, which must never be undermined. Thus, humanity will not tolerate any more attempts to disregard human dignity and it has the right to intervene whenever this value is in danger.

The developments in the area of humanitarian international law and consequently the introduction – for the first time ever – of the concept of international criminal justice[7] (apart from the International Court of Justice only dealing with states) reflect the new idea that individuals are also actors in international law and can be effectively treated by it. With those developments – and many others – the states finally lost, once and for all, the ability to govern their own affairs internally, if to do so violates fundamental principles and humanitarian laws. To take an example, humanitarian law would give the right to anyone[8] to intervene in Yugoslavia during critical times of genocide, and international criminal law would acquire the power to bring to court Presidents of the Republic having immunity both under their national constitutions and under customary international law.

---

[6] See any textbook of international law, extended bibliography in the 1920s and 1930s, and, among others: JE Harley, *The League of Nations and the New International Law* (New York, Oxford University Press, 1921); G Scott, *Rise and Fall of the League of Nations* (London, Hutchinson, 1973); RB Henig (ed), *The League of Nations* (Edinburgh, Oliver and Boyd, 1973).

[7] See among others, B Broomhall, *International Justice and the International Criminal Court: Between Sovereignty and the Rule of Law* (Oxford, Oxford University Press, 2003); J Dugard and C Van de Wyngaert (eds), *International Criminal Law and Procedure* (Aldershot, Dartmouth, 1996); K Lescure, *International Justice for Former Yugoslavia, the Working of the International Criminal Tribunal of the Hague* (The Hague, London, Kluwer, 1996); LN Sadat, *The International Criminal Court and the Transformation of International Law, Justice for the New Millennium* (Ardsley NY, Transnational Publishers, 2002); D Shelton (ed), *International Crimes, Peace, and Human Rights, the Role of the International Criminal Court* (Ardsley NY, Transnational Publishers, 2000); P Sands, *From Nuremberg to the Hague, the Future of International Criminal Justice* (Cambridge, Cambridge University Press, 2003).

[8] Following the action taken by Bernard Kouchner for revealing the genocide in Bosnia-Herzegovina and the initiatives of his organization 'Doctors of the World' (Médecins du Monde) in the region.

International law developed in this environment, and it continues to develop in all directions. In the main, this is through the initiatives of the main political international organizations, but it is also via the thousands of treaties signed and ratified on a continuous basis by states and international organizations. This process – embracing both objectives and solutions to them – continues to flourish around the world.[9]

International law was therefore easily fragmented in the sense that every area of its development took its own path and produced its own, hitherto unseen, results. Despite this, international law conserves its initial integrating force, around the values that it serves and represents. As a result of this defining integrating power, modern international law is becoming the cradle of nascent ideas, initiatives, strategies and interventions, changing the world and consequently the realities and the legal concept of state. The role of courts at the international or supranational level is significant in promoting unity.[10]

In very practical terms the changes in the realities and legal concept of state occur, inter alia, in the following ways.

In the case of the Western European states, a major change was introduced after the Second World War, the creation of which evolved into what we know as the European Union. This institution already had mechanisms to encourage an ongoing integration of its Member States, which have gradually lost competences in favour of what have been called supranational institutions. In the current state of the European Union, almost all sectors of public activity reflect the importance and presence of European law; there are no customs between the states, there is free movement of people and goods and most importantly, almost nothing is decided by the states without prior consultation with their partners or without taking the others into consideration.

Similar experiments with integration are advanced in various regions of the world, with similar or lower levels of success. This is particularly the case in the

---

[9] A central characteristic of the new era in the development of public international law is the internationalization of public law. Traditional constitutional law, especially the values promoted in the fields of civil liberties, the welfare state and judicial protection, but also state organization, are coming into international law and have developed in new ways through it. At the same time, traditional international law is vigorously entering into internal public law and becomes one of the sources of internal legality of the state action. It needs to be taken into consideration that, in many countries of modern times, international law is lent (by the constitutions themselves) a rank superior to the Acts of Parliament or even of the Constitution itself. The international standards of state conduct have become internal state law. See, on this point: *Internationalization of Public Law – Proceedings of the European Group of Public Law Conference 2005*, European Public Law Series vol LXXXIII (London, Esperia, 2004).

[10] The issue is part of the broader discussion on the fragmentation of international law, an idea which has been heavily promoted in the last 20 years. This fragmentation was the result of the sudden and unprecedented development of various sectors of international law, which produced the impression of losing their reference to central ideas and values. As international law and globalization continue to progress, it becomes obvious that there is a central system of values and principles in international law, which is serving as the connecting element of a continuously growing area of legal order. This is also served by the proliferation of international courts, which bring to unity the solid ground that it deserves. See also: S Cassese, *When Legal Orders Collide: The Role of Courts* (Global Law Press, Editoria Derecho Global, 2010).

area of integration of the markets or of defence policies. At the same time, the World Trade Organization (WTO) has produced rules and mechanisms for the regulation of international trade in a world increasingly engaging in commerce without frontiers. Although the scope of the organization is, necessarily, currently a pipe dream, the WTO is rapidly advancing into producing legal principles and practices of worldwide importance and applicability, through which the globe will be more and more homogenized.

As all international organizations are obliged to offer their staff members an up-to-date system of legal protection which, at the very least, reflects the level of quality offered by participating states (and especially that of the state of the head-quarters), they have gradually developed sophisticated grievance systems. Those systems, in response to the high level of legal science of the states, have developed in their own right and taken their own path. In this way, they have produced rules and practices from the common standards of a worldwide civilization, and, in their turn, widely reflect legal knowledge and best practice.[11]

Nowadays, however, there are international organizations which were conceived as, or developed into, couriers of modern rules and best practices to be followed by the states. These include, for example, the World Bank, the International Monetary Fund (IMF), the OECD (Organization for Economic Co-operation and Development), and many others focusing on specific areas of state activities. Quite often, these international organizations have neither the means nor the will to impose such rules or best practices around the world by direct coercion; all the same, they develop their own ways for successfully promoting them.

One illustrative example of this is when, for instance, the World Bank offers a loan or supports the execution of a project somewhere in the world, it may – if it sees fit – attach a reform agenda to the project. Thus, unless best practices are adopted by the given state, the project will not produce its desired effects. Moreover, specialized organs of the World Bank or the World Bank Group have been created and are imposed upon the contracting states as mandatory jurisdictions in areas such as the protection of the environment, or litigation with private entrepreneurial partners in the execution of a given project.

The same rules apply for the IMF which always attaches a mandatory reform project to its loans for supporting state economies. These are supposed to guarantee the stability of the state after the crisis which necessitated the IMF intervention.

This way of advancing reforms has become common practice. Moreover, in parallel with it, the OECD is also promoting reforms independently, so that the states are continuously at the level expected in modern times. In addition, the OECD has its own indirect ways of imposing its reasoning upon the states, especially through periodical reviews.

---

[11] See, among others: S Flogaitis, 'I principi generali del diritto nella giurisprudenza del Tribunale Amministrativo delle Nazioni Unite' in M d'Alberti (ed), *Le nuove mete del diritto amministrativo* (Bologna, Il Mulino, 2010) 93; also, United Nations Administrative Tribunal, *International Administrative Tribunals in a Changing World* (London, Esperia, 2008).

A very interesting evolution in recent times is the development of what was called administration by networks.[12] Of course, the creation of networks – either regionally or internationally – is not a novelty. On the contrary, all metropolitan legal systems have traditionally developed networks of institutions and people in the countries of their interest or influence, especially through 'international' associations, regrouping representatives of the metropolitan country and through friends of its culture from other countries. This practice could have lost some of its effectiveness with globalization, which has opened the doors in the creation of institutional or personal networks of all sorts, many of them very influential.

Examples of institutional networks are the International Association of High Courts, or of High Administrative Courts, or of European state courts, among others. They constitute quasi-official platforms of mutual influence in terms of ways of thinking (or in other ways) and contribute indirectly to the advancement of the idea of homogenization in the fields of their interest, without the state being able to influence, either positively or negatively.

Some institutional networks are constituted by international treaties and have more direct results, because they always bypass central state powers. This is the case, for instance, of the institutional cooperation between the antitrust authorities of the European Union, all of them independent from the central government, or of the network of the central banks of the Member States of the European Union. More important, although comparatively covert, are all sorts of institutional networks created by law or soft law in the areas of policing, combating money laundering, human trafficking and terrorism, among others.

The networks created by individuals are no less interesting, especially because nowadays, they mostly operate under the cloak of powerful NGOs. The effects of these networks have ramifications all over the world and they exploit direct access to the press and mass media. An example of their powerful effect is that the action of one of them against the genocide in the former Yugoslavia not only changed the political situation of that country but proved to be the prelude to NATO (North Atlantic Treaty Organization) intervention and the opportunity for the general acceptance of the principle that – in cases of genocide – anyone can respond and save human dignity.

Freedom of expression – with its ramifications for the freedom of the press, including the mass media – was a key factor for determining the evolution from the one-class to the multi-class state, and the same can be said of it today. This is especially true in the case of television, which can and does broadcast around the globe in seconds. This means that broadcasters can choose any information or

---

[12] S Cassese, *Lo spazio giurdico globale* (Roma, Laterza, 2003) 21; G Thompson et al (eds), *Markets, Hierarchies and Networks, the Coordination of Social Life* (London, Sage, 1991); WJM Kickert et al (eds), *Managing Complex Networks* (London, Sage, 1997); P Bogason and TAJ Toonen, 'Introduction: Networks in Public Administration' (1998) 76 *Public Administration* 205; TAJ Toonen, 'Networks, Management and Institutions: Public Administration as "Normal Science"' (1998) 76 *Public Administration* 229.

political message, without being subject to the laws of the receiving country and – inevitably – these are beyond the control of their government.

We could continue endlessly enumerating initiatives, which are taken without necessarily following a global plan; they are – in reality – necessary responses to real problems which arise because of the new globalized environment and new technologies, and so on, and they are mostly *ad hoc* measures, contributing – at least at first – to even more fragmentation of the global legal space. From the existence of, and the international role of the agencies rating national economies, to the new institutions created or promoted by the United Nations for the combat of international terrorism, the global legal space has come to the attention of all public lawyers. They are called upon to study it and integrate it. In such development, and depending on the case, the states may or may not function as the promoting catalysts of the new phenomenon. It could therefore be seen as ironic that, at one and the same time, they are also circumvented by it.

The Reaction of the State, Crises, Reforms and the Gradual Constellation of Multi-level Public Power, both Nationally and Internationally

As paradoxical as it might appear, the only way for the states to face the result of that rapid evolution, is to contribute to creating more and more institutions and international rules promoting integration of the international law and environment, in other words, the creation of a robust global legal space. Unfortunately, this simultaneously means a less coherent state, which could be seen as the victim of a lent process of deconstruction in the global legal space.

From an institutional point of view, the following tendencies characterize the states' evolution since the end of the Second World War:

The first is the reinforcement of the executive with regards to Parliament, in the field of rulemaking. All constitutions are characterized by the wish clearly and efficiently to regulate the rulemaking powers of the executive. The latter acquired a well-defined role in the rulemaking process and has become, for the first time since the French Revolution, equal partner in rulemaking with the parliaments. If we take into consideration the quantities of legislation produced, in many cases it can be said that the primary legislator was the executive, with its rulemaking authority very often deriving directly from the constitutions themselves.

The executive was reinforced in relation to the parliaments which shared the field of political governance. Starting with the Fundamental Law of Bonn of 1948, one after another, the constitutions presented a clear pattern of helping governments to stay in power, despite the difficulties they might have had in the national parliaments. An original idea of *in dubio* in favour of governmental stability was gradually developed in the political and legal environments of contemporary states. This was often coupled with the introduction of electoral systems which reinforced the chances of the first party to form a government.

The idea behind this evolution is that the most important attribute of the political system is not the political in-fighting between factions of a society, which is so often played out within parliaments, but the strength of governance. This is because strong governments are thought to be the best protectors of the development of political systems, democratic principles, and the many goals of modern civilization. Parliaments are thus fading in importance and are becoming merely instrumental in the canvas of features securing governance.

Furthermore, public administration is now working under the close scrutiny of the judges, no matter whether the chosen system is of a unitary or dual jurisdiction. When administrative law was first produced by the French Revolution, it was powerful machinery, and intended to be outside any extrinsic control. Nowadays, public administration is operated under the strict control of the law, by the judges who have become institutionally and – in the public opinion – the best warrantors of democracy, substituted in the sovereign nation's historic role.[13]

In this context, the executive, comprising public administration and the political personnel of the government, once more becomes the spine of the state, its main power – as it was before the French Revolution in the state of absolutism. This time, however, it has a new democratic legitimacy. At the same time, the judiciary becomes the warrantor of the people's interests in a democratic society. The reform of public administration has therefore become an issue of constant concern to modern societies and states, including the administration of the judicial system.

The major reform platform which was proposed after the 1980s was New Public Management. It advanced the following policies for public administration:[14]

a) *Agencification*, in other words, the organizational scheme in which public services, instead of being governed by the central administrative apparatus, are entrusted to specialized agencies created for that purpose.

b) *Process re-engineering*, in other words, revision of the administrative procedures with the scope to make them more efficient and citizen-friendly.

c) *Value for money*, in other words, better productivity of public services, with lower costs, in the same way as in any other private business.

d) *Result-oriented budget*, in order to reinforce the value for money process.

e) *Public–private partnership*, in the sense of bringing the private sector into the public administration, either through procedures of contracting out, or by

---

[13] Among others, Brunella Casalini, 'Sovranità popolare, governo della legge e governo dei giudici negli Stati Uniti di America' in Costa and Zolo (eds), *Lo Stato di diritto*, above n 1 at 224.

[14] Following Cassese, *Lo spazio giuridico globale*, above n 12 at 168; also, among others, FF Ridley, 'The New Public Management in Europe, Comparative Perspectives' (1996) 11 *Public Policy and Administration* 16; F Naschold, *New Frontiers in Public Sector Management: Trends and Issues in State and Local Government in Europe* (Berlin, W de Gruyter, 1996); T Younis et al, 'The Application of Total Quality Management to the Public Sector' (1996) 62 *International Review of Administrative Sciences* 369; WJM Kickert (ed), *Public Management and Administrative Reform in Western Europe* (Cheltenham, Edward Elgar, 1997); JA Desveaux, *Designing Bureaucracies* (Stanford, Stanford University Press, 1995).

entrusting entire public services or public goods for development to private business.

f) *Marketization*, in other words, the introduction of market principles in public administration, especially the idea of competition.

g) *Customer orientation*, in other words, taking into account the need for satisfaction of the user of public services with the same criteria of any private business.

For the first time ever, reforms were not driven by the rule of law and its needs, nor by the idea that public services need to work because this was needed for the general interest. This time, the public services had to be reorganized and procedures had to be reinvented. This was always to be achieved with an awareness of what private businesses do in order to be successful, and with the implied, but not declared, will to help the private initiative to create new wealth through the new style of partnership with the state.

New Public Management was, and is, an important step in the development of administrative science, because it brought a fresh point of view into a domain which was traditionally seen as the realm of public law and lawyers. This new viewpoint derived from economics and from theories of corporate governance. The excesses of the new doctrine, however, brought difficulties to modern states as, for example, in the times of fluxes in New Orleans, or on 11 September, both having led to an important return to traditional ways of organizing public services. The same happened in the states of Central and Eastern Europe after the fall of the Berlin wall, where it became obvious that what was urgently needed was not New Public Management but the rule of law and practicality-based training of public officials on what this meant.

Developments regarding the provision and state supervision of public utilities offer a perfect illustration of the above evolution. After a long period of 'suffocating', and off-market state control of such activities, it became obvious,[15] mainly in the USA and the UK, that this organizational model was rather ineffective. In order to cure 'regulatory failures', neo-liberal administration in those countries decided to perform extensive *de-regulation* and *privatization* of those industries (telecoms, energy, transport) without avoiding some excesses.[16]

In the European Union, the new model for the services of general economic interest,[17] as designed by the EU, is markedly different. Whilst acknowledging the inefficiencies of the traditional, 'agoraphobic'[18] approach of the French scholars

---

[15] Under the influence of the New Chicago School led by scholars, such as R Posner, who use economic analysis to answer legal questions.

[16] Such as the energy blackouts in California, during the summer of 2000. See B Du Marais, *Droit public de la régulation économique* (Presses de Sciences Po, Dalloz, 2004) 561; and R Cudahy, 'Electric Deregulation after California: Down but Not Out' (2002) *Administrative Law Review* 333.

[17] This term is used in the treaties of the EU and encompasses the activities defined as '*services publics*' in France, '*Daseinvorsorge*' in Germany and 'public utilities' or 'public services' in Great Britain.

[18] Literally, the term agoraphobic means fear 'φόβος/phobos' for the market 'αγορά/agora'. See G Dellis, 'Régulation et droit public "continental". Essai d'une approche synthétique' (2010) *Revue de Droit Public* 957.

regarding the *services publics*, the EU promotes, not the deregulation but the *liberalization* of those activities, in other words, their gradual opening to market rules and conditions, without undermining their social importance. Rather than leading to the extinction of state control, this leads to a new, market-oriented, public regulation,[19] following the principles of networks administration and New Public Management.[20] A century after Léon Duguit,[21] his concept of public service has not been abandoned but modernized in a more market-friendly manner, following the evolution of the state and mutations of public law in a globalized economic environment.[22]

The Dilution of the States in the International Environment and the Rule of Law

Today, we are witnessing a dilution of the states in the international global space, both legally and institutionally. At the same time, we see their continuous effort to become able – through reform – to respond to new realities and challenges. The states continue declaring themselves based on the doctrines and practices which gave rise to them. The truth is, however, that the re-engineered state of modern times is more oriented towards concerns for political stability and efficiency, than to its own adaptation to the global legal space.

As the global legal space develops – fragmented, polycentric and empirical – new roles and new sciences are emerging depicting pictures never before seen which, in their turn, contribute to the creation of a new unity. This is one served by the judges and their case law, internationally but also nationally and by the global administrative law, called to develop the principles and values of global importance, and drawn from all sorts of administrative events and so bringing a

---

[19] The common use of the term regulation, in almost all languages, (*régulation, Regulierung, regolazione*) reflects this new relationship between the state, public law and the markets.

[20] eg the organizational model for liberalized sectors such as electronic communication, energy and gas is the following: the provision of the service is open to new entrants, after the abolition of the exclusive rights that were granted to public or private monopolies. Alternative operators have the right to access the required networks and are protected against former monopolies through a set of specific rules, which aim to create a competitive environment. At the same time, the general interest is preserved through duties imposed upon operators in the form of 'universal service' obligations that ensure access of all potential users to a minimum standard of service, even in cases where the free market is unable to ensure such a minimum. The proper functioning of the sector is safeguarded by public regulators, established in the form of independent administrative authorities, which combine economic expertise and private methods with public law. Since those sectors exceed national level, their cross-border regulation is achieved through a cooperation network of the national regulators (see, eg the Agency for the Cooperation of Energy Regulators (ACER)) under the high authority of the European Commission. See I Walden (ed), *Telecommunications Law and Regulation,* 4th edn (Oxford, Oxford University Press, 2012); K Talus, *EU Energy Law and Policy. A Critical Account* (Oxford, Oxford University Press, 2013) and Du Marais, above n 16.

[21] See above, Lesson 6.

[22] Dellis, 'Régulation et droit public "continental"' above n 18 at 957.

homogenized civilization of a new public administration and of a fresh concept of state.

Moreover, legal civilization for what concerns the exercise of public power is returning to where it started, to the rule of law, the concept with the remarkable and unprecedented *iter*, finding its roots in England centuries ago. After having conquered the world of the states, it has become the connecting element of the world created by the states, in other words, of the new international law.

Conclusions

The concept of state developed gradually from the middle of the fourteenth century, in parallel with the decline of the imperial dream. Historically, this tendency had already started in the twelfth century, especially in South-Western Europe, mostly with the city–states of the Italian peninsula. This was something that indicated that the closer and more exposed the western societies were to the late Roman Empire, the quicker they absorbed certain ideas from the East and introduced reform, leading to the concept of state and with multiplying effects on the others.

The state's glorious times were mainly the eighteenth and the nineteenth centuries, because in that period they became rationalized, well organized, and powerful and were respected by both citizens and the international world. During those years – but also in the twentieth century – the political fights for democracy for all, together with wars, have led to the creation of modern societies and institutions with regards to public powers.

This is the kind of state that for scholastic reasons we continue to teach about in law faculties. At the same time, it is common knowledge that this state does not exist anymore, nor is it ever likely to appear again, because the states have created an international community, composed of states and international organizations, but also of all sorts of other international players, including individuals.

International law – a sort of annex to any law faculty teaching around 40 years ago, and taught by a mere handful of scholars forming something approaching an exclusive club – has, in recent years, witnessed an unprecedented expansion. Constitutional and administrative law have largely contributed to that development and enrichment of international law which, freshly invigorated, has made a grand entrance into the internal life of modern states, imposing new standards of law, behaviour and ways of exercising public power. Modern instruments of international law, especially the Bretton Woods institutions and their far-reaching spirit, the fight against terrorism, human trafficking and money laundering, international humanitarian law, and so on, are creating a new world with no frontiers to them, where the state is but one of the players. Moreover, in most instances, the state is internally diluted and considerably fragmented; elements and institutions coexist with it rather than existing because of it, alongside constitutions adopted in the period starting with the end of the Second World War.

In this new world, the judges are institutionally upwardly-mobile – mainly in the public consciousness – in the position of warrantors of the democratic principle and the fundamental values of our civilization, internally for the states and in the international arena. The balance is shifting from the struggle for democracy to the belief that the values should have their realm above and beyond nations and states, under the warranty of the servants of the law.

Index